THE
MAN
WHO
WALKED
THROUGH
TIME

ALSO BY COLIN FLETCHER

The Secret Worlds of Colin Fletcher (1989)

The Complete Walker III (1984)

The Man from the Cave (1981)

The New Complete Walker (1974)

The Winds of Mara (1973)

The Complete Walker (1968)

The Thousand-Mile Summer (1964)

Colin Fletcher

—

THE
MAN
WHO
WALKED
THROUGH
TIME

VINTAGE BOOKS

A DIVISION OF RANDOM HOUSE, INC.

NEW YORK

*There is a relation between the hours of our life and
the centuries of time. . . . The hours should be instructed
by the ages, and the ages explained by the hours.*

—EMERSON

Vintage Books Edition, May 1989

Text copyright © 1967 by Colin Fletcher

All rights reserved under International and Pan-American Copyright Conventions. Published in the United States by Random House, Inc., New York, and simultaneously in Canada by Random House of Canada Limited, Toronto. Originally published by Alfred A. Knopf, Inc., on January 15, 1968.

Library of Congress Cataloging in Publication Data
Fletcher, Colin.
The man who walked through time.
1. Grand Canyon.   I. Title.
[F788.F55 1972]   917.91'32'045   72-4082
ISBN 0-679-72306-4 (pbk.)

Book design by Jennifer Dossin

Map copyright © 1989 by Claudia Carlson

Manufactured in the United States of America
10 9 8

CONTENTS

———

THE PLACE   3

THE DREAM   5

THE JOURNEY   15

Entrance   15
Reconnaissance   27
Interlude   46
Challenge   56
Transition   87
Rock   103
Rhythm   112
Life   149
Man   179
Exit   222

EPILOGUE   233

APPENDIX   243

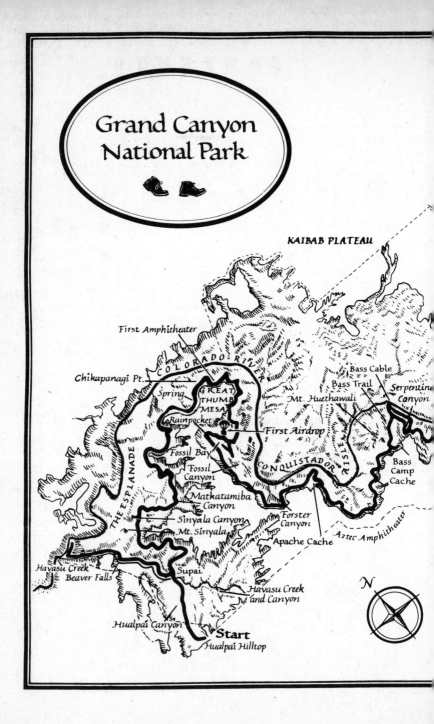

Grand Canyon
National Park

KAIBAB PLATEAU

First Amphitheater

Chikapanagi Pt.

COLORADO RIVER

Spring

GREAT THUMB MESA

Rainpocket

First Airdrop

Bass Cable

Bass Trail

Serpentine Canyon

Mt. Huethawali

Fossil Bay

Fossil Canyon

CONQUISTADOR

Bass Camp Cache

Matkatamiba Canyon

THE ESPLANADE

Sinyala Canyon

Mt. Sinyala

Forster Canyon

Apache Cache

Aztec Amphitheater

Havasu Creek

Beaver Falls

Supai

Havasu Creek and Canyon

N

Hualpai Canyon

Start
Hualpai Hilltop

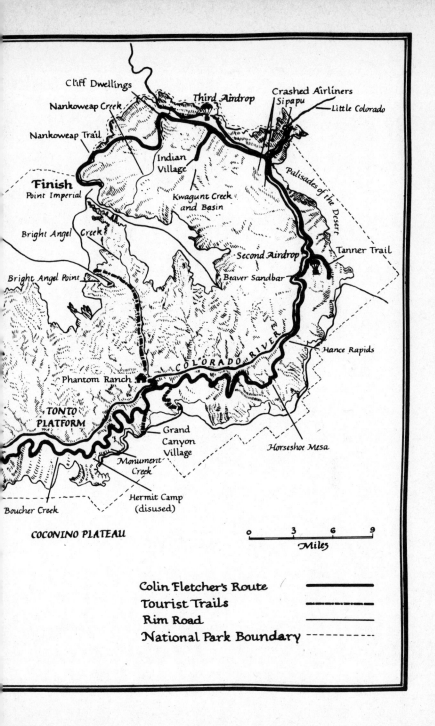

Cliff Dwellings

Nankoweap Creek

Nankoweap Trail

Finish
Point Imperial

Bright Angel Creek

Bright Angel Point

Phantom Ranch

**TONTO
PLATFORM**

Boucher Creek

COCONINO PLATEAU

Third Airdrop

Crashed Airliners
Sipapu

Little Colorado

Indian
Village

Kwagunt Creek
and Basin

Palisades of the Desert

Second Airdrop

Beaver Sandbar

Tanner Trail

C O L O R A D O   R I V E R

Hance Rapids

Grand
Canyon
Village

Monument
Creek

Horseshoe Mesa

Hermit Camp
(disused)

0   3   6   9
Miles

Colin Fletcher's Route
Tourist Trails
Rim Road
National Park Boundary

THE
MAN
WHO
WALKED
THROUGH
TIME

TIME NOTE

A quarter of a century ago, when I made this journey, Grand Canyon was largely untraveled below its Rims. So I did certain things that at the time seemed legitimate. I lit occasional campfires, for example. I had three supply drops parachuted from lowflying aircraft. I killed a rattlesnake. I slept inside an Anasazi cliff dwelling.

I hope you will understand that because of today's heavy travel in the Canyon by backpackers and river-runners such acts would now be neither legitimate nor legal.

C.F.
1990

THE PLACE

———

IT WOULD probably be a good thing to look first at some hard, objective facts.

The Grand Canyon of the Colorado is a chasm that slices through the plateau country of northern Arizona like a gigantic and impossible desert crevasse. It is more than two hundred river-miles long. At its center it is over a mile deep: if you built four Empire State Buildings in it, one on top of the other, they would not rise level with the Rim. The Canyon averages ten miles across, but some of its bays swing back for twenty, thirty, even forty miles. In all it covers more than one thousand square miles. But the vast bulk of this area is almost never visited. Even today, unexplored corners remain.

The story of how the Canyon came into being is quite simple.

A long time ago—for the moment, let us call it seven million years ago—the Colorado River meandered across a plain. Then a huge dome began to push up, very slowly, in the river's path. As the dome rose, an inch a century perhaps, the river cut down into it. That is all. No sudden cataclysm. Just an immensely slow adjustment to new conditions, on an immense scale and over immense spans of time. An adjustment that is probably still going on. Today, the Colorado runs in much the same place as it did before the dome began to rise. But the rocks that seven million years ago bordered its banks now form the Canyon's rim, a vertical mile above the river.*

It is easy enough, of course, to grasp this story with your intellect. The difficulty comes when you try to accept its reality with your whole being, as completely as you accept that a very old man has lived for almost a century. And in the Canyon even this acceptance is only a beginning.

Most of us, when we first think deeply about such time spans, tend to draw back in fear from their brink, just as we tend at first to draw back in fear from the brink of anything so immense as Grand Canyon. But it is worth remembering, I think, that some element of fear probably lies at the root of every substantial challenge. And it makes no difference at all whether the challenge is to your mind or to your body, or whether—with richer promise than either, alone—it embraces both.

*See Update, page 240.

THE DREAM

———

IT HAPPENED quite unexpectedly, the way the big
moments often do. A friend and I were driving from
New York to the West Coast in early June, and we
had detoured north from US 66 for a hurried look at
Grand Canyon. It was midmorning when we parked
the car and walked across asphalt toward the Rim. I
had seen my quota of photographs and paintings, of
course, and thought I knew what to expect: an impressive view that no self-respecting tourist ought to
miss.

Long before we came close, I saw the space. A huge,
cleaving space that the photographs and paintings had
done nothing to prepare me for. An impossible,
breath-taking gap in the face of the earth. And up from
this void shone a soft, luminous light.

We came to the lip of the Rim.

And there, defeating my senses, was the depth. The
depth and the distances. Cliffs and buttes and hanging
terraces, all sculptured on a scale beyond anything I
had ever imagined. Colors neither red nor white nor
pink nor purple but a fusion. And stamped across everything, the master pattern.

Even before I had accepted what I saw, I heard the silence; felt it, like something solid, face to face. A silence in which the squawk of a blue jay was sacrilege. A silence so profound that the whole colossal chaos of rock and space and color seemed to have sunk beneath it and to lie there cut off, timeless.

In that first moment of shock, with my mind already exploding beyond old boundaries, I knew that something had happened to the way I looked at things.

Oddly enough, I am no longer quite sure when the decision came. It was not, I know, during the first morning. But all afternoon I sat on the Rim and looked down into the burning and apparently waterless waste of rock. Looked more closely now at the master pattern that is the fabric of the Canyon. At the layered, sawtooth pattern that had leaped out at me, simple and striking, in that first moment of shock. I looked at its huge, alternating bands of cliff and hanging terrace that reach down, repeating but never repititious, from Rim almost to river. I looked east and west, as far as my eyes could strain, until cliff and terrace tapered away into hazy distances. It was mysterious and terrible—and beckoning. And some time during the afternoon, as I sat on the brink of this strange new world, it came to me that if a route existed I would walk from one end of the Canyon to the other. Once the idea had crystallized, no hideously sensible doubts reared up to plague me. And I did not need such fragile props as "reasons." The only question I asked myself was whether the project would turn out to be physically possible. Perhaps it is in this kind of simple certainty that most of the world's ridiculous and wonderful dreams are born.*

---

*It occurs to me that my decision may need some kind of background explanation. I am what might be called a compulsive walker. Any free week end I am liable to pick up a road map, choose a large, blank area that

Late in the afternoon of that first day I went to the National Park Visitor Center. There I learned that although many people had run the river in boats, no one seemed to have forced a passage of the Canyon on foot. I was still aware, I think, only of the physical challenge of what I had seen, and the questions I asked were severely practical. I wanted to know, for example, whether it was possible for a man to make his way along those steep hanging terraces. (I have called them hanging terraces because that was how they immediately struck me; but perhaps I should explain that they are narrow, steeply sloping ledges that often extend for mile after mile after mile as precarious steps between successive cliff faces.) I also wanted to know whether water existed, here and there, down in that world of heat and dryness. But beyond the fact that people had died of thirst there, even in recent years, the only important thing I found out for certain was that nobody seemed to know very much about such matters. Yet as I strolled around the Visitor Center and studied its exhibits and talked to park rangers I learned many new facts. I learned about the vegetation that grows down in what your eye reports from the Rim as a wasteland of bare rock. (It is only distance that has canceled the signs of life.) I learned about the many animals that live in that "dead" world: not only spiders and rattlesnakes, but deer and coyotes and bobcats and even mountain lions. I learned about the fossils, those messages from the ancient past. About the rocks. And about their meanings. And after a while, reaching out at least beyond mere in-

---

intrigues me, drive to the edge of it, park my car, walk in with a pack on my back, and find out what's there. Once, on something suspiciously like impulse, I spent a summer walking from one end of California to the other—from Mexico to Oregon. In six months I walked well over a thousand miles, through deserts and mountains. And I have never for a moment regretted it.

formation, I grasped that the Canyon is a huge natural museum of the earth's history.

That evening I escaped from the crowded places—from the asphalt and its automobiles, from tourists harnessed to their cameras, from hotel porters in garish red jackets—and walked along an unfrequented stretch of the Rim. I sat down under a juniper tree. And in that quiet place I found that I had moved inside the silence.

When I had sat and looked for a long time at the tremendous expanse of rock sculpture spread out below me, I began to understand, more than just intellectually, something of how it had become sculpture. And I began to understand that the silence was not, as I had thought, a timeless silence. It was a silence built of the seconds that had ticked away, eon after eon, as certainly and deliberately as our seconds tick past today. Just for a moment I glimpsed the centuries reaching back and down into the Canyon and into the past, back and down through the corridor of time that stretches silently away behind us, back and down into the huge history that seems at first to leave no meaningful place for man.

And presently, when the fear had begun to subside, I saw that my decision to walk through the Canyon could mean more than I knew. I saw that by going down into that huge fissure in the face of the earth, deep into the space and the silence and the solitude, I might come as close as we can at present to moving back and down through the smooth and apparently impenetrable face of time. If I could contribute enough, the journey might teach me in the end, with a certainty no book can give, how the centuries have built the world we know. For I would see how the rocks had been constructed, and how they had been carved. How life had mushroomed from simple beginnings into the complex and astonishing pageant we now accept so casually. How it had covered the rocks with a web whose intricate and interlocking structure all too often becomes invisible to us "civilized" and estranged people. I would see many strands from this web: simple algae and lichens as well as juniper trees; catfish and butterflies and hummingbirds as well as wild horses and bighorn sheep and other members of that mammalian strand of life which has recently come to dominate the world's fabric. I would even find traces of the self-conscious mammal that has, for the last little cupful of centuries, multiplied its numbers and its complexities so prodigiously that it threatens, any minute now, to tear apart the whole delicately balanced structure and leave only tattered remnants trembling in the winds of time. I might even glimpse some hint of how this curious animal fits meaningfully into the broader scheme. I might find—beyond our present intellectual answers, but in harmony with them—some kind of new personal solution to man's ancient and continuing conundrums: "Where do we come from?" "What are we doing here?" For by living close to the web of life and to the foundations across which it stretches I might in the end gain some tentative insight into the pattern on which both have been built.

I did not understand, there under the juniper tree, how this vision would fit into my own small life. But it did not matter. I understood enough.

A year passed before I could start my journey.

Perhaps it was just as well: there is no test quite like the erosion of time for finding out whether you really want to do something. If the dream you have dreamed can survive untarnished through a year of doubt and discouragement and frustration and all the drawn-out detail of research and planning and preparation, then you can safely assume that you want to go through with the project.

Quite early in that intervening year it became obvious that "from one end of Grand Canyon to the other" had been a fuzzy target; no two people seemed able to agree about where the Canyon began and ended. So I refocused. I would walk "from one end of Grand Canyon National Park to the other"—the Canyon's major and most magnificent part.

As the months passed I harvested all the practical information I could raise. It was a thin crop. I found, with one notable exception, no one who could help me very much. But I consulted excellent topographical maps, fairly complete weather statistics, and a couple of marginally informative old exploration reports. And slowly I found my outline answers.

I would set aside two months for the journey. I knew that I could probably force a passage through the Canyon considerably faster, but to do so would mean making my journey a battle. And what I wanted, if I could manage it, was something closer to a picnic. Or perhaps I mean a pilgrimage.

As I had expected, the obvious route along the Colorado was almost certainly out: the river often cut, mile after mile, through deep gorges that everyone agreed were impassable on foot. But the hanging terraces sometimes broadened into rock platforms, and even where they pinched in to steep and narrow talus (a sloping mass of loose rock fragments), it seemed probable that in most places a man could pick his way along them.

The big barrier, I confirmed, was water. In the

Park's eastern half I would often be able to get down quite easily to the Colorado. There were also several permanent sidecreeks. But in the western section the river ran through an almost continuous gorge, rarely accessible from above, and I would have to rely mostly on rainpockets—small rockpools of rain or melted snow. Heavy rainshowers usually fell in late summer, but they were extremely erratic, and by then temperatures deep in the Canyon would on most days be over 100 degrees in the shade. A more reliable time for rain or snow was winter and early spring. But winter temperatures might fall almost as low as the 22 degrees below zero once recorded on the South Rim, and that is no weather for a pilgrimage, let alone a picnic. So I decided to start in early April. It seemed to me that if I planned efficiently, carried two gallons of water, did nothing foolish, and studiously avoided bad luck, I ought to get by.

I knew that even with a sixty-pound load on my back I could carry only one week's food at a time, so I decided to send one week's supply down by mule train to the Indian village of Supai, and another week's to Phantom Ranch, the only other inhabited place in the Canyon. I would also plant out two caches. And I would charter three parachute airdrops.

The supplies for both caches and drops would be packed in five-gallon metal cans. In addition to a week's dehydrated rations (spiced by one can of delicacies, such as oysters or frogs' legs, and a small bottle of claret) each can would contain such vital replacements as white gas for the cooking stove, toilet paper, bookmatches, film, flashlight batteries, detergent powder, soap (half a bar), boot wax, onionskin paper for notes, rubbing alcohol for refreshing and hardening feet, and spare plastic freezer bags in various sizes for protecting almost everything. Some cans would also include socks, foot powder, and water-purifying tablets.

In the final month of the year of waiting, with preparations mounting to their inevitable climax, every day pulsated with problems: Grappling with the huge, multiple-minuscule issues of what equipment to take and what to leave behind. Deciding what to do about such hazards as rattlesnakes, scorpions, and twisted ankles miles from water. Discovering desperately late in the day that there simply wasn't enough money in the bank to see the thing through—and then, at half past the eleventh hour, having the best-paying magazine in the country buy one of my stories.

At last the final problems sank away and it was time to go, and I loaded everything into my old station wagon and drove the eight hundred miles from my apartment in Berkeley, California, to Flagstaff, Arizona, where I had some last-minute administrative details to tie down.

I do not think I ever really considered that things might go seriously wrong. I am still naïve enough to believe that if a man wants something badly enough he usually gets it. And I still wanted the Canyon. Wanted it badly.

Naturally, I had done all I could to keep it that way—to keep my dream fresh and untarnished, to shield it at all costs from familiarity, that sly and deadly anesthetic.

For one thing, I had decided after careful consideration that, except for some simple geology, I would do very little reading about the Canyon—no more than seemed necessary to extract vital information about routes and water sources. After all, I was not going down into the Canyon to learn intellectual facts.

I took similar precautions with the Canyon itself. On my first brief visit I had walked down a well-used tourist trail until I was several hundred feet below the Rim. What I saw had horrified and humbled and entranced me. It had been all the preview I needed; and I soon understood that it was also all I could allow. Later, in the planning stages, several people had said: "Why not fly over beforehand, low? That's the way to choose a safe route." But I had resisted the temptation.

When it came to siting the two food caches a delicate problem arose: I knew that if I packed stores down into the Canyon I would be "trespassing" in what I wanted to be unknown country; but I also knew that if I planted my caches outside the Rim I would in picking them up break both the real and symbolic continuity of my journey. In the end I solved the dilemma by siting each cache a few feet below the Rim.

Finally, when I had to hang around Grand Canyon Village for almost two weeks because of an infected heel, I went to the Rim no more than two or three times. Even then I took care to look only at the surface of what I saw.

And it worked. My dream survived.

Then, late one mid-April day, the dream faded quietly away and the reality was born.

Grand Canyon Geology, *Simplified Profile (Schematic)*

RIM		*Average thickness, in feet*	*Current estimate of age, in millions of years*
	LIMESTONE (gray-white)	400	225
	SANDSTONE (pale brown)	350	250
	SUPAI FORMATION — SHALES AND SANDSTONES (red)	1,000	275
ESPLANADE	THE REDWALL — LIMESTONE (blue-gray, stained red)	600	300
	MUAV LIMESTONE (gray, stained red)	200	450
TONTO PLATFORM	BRIGHT ANGEL SHALE (layered, greenish gray/purple)	600	475
INNER GORGE	TAPEATS SANDSTONE (brown)	225	500
	Erosion Surface — The Great Unconformity		
	SCHISTS (dark gray — with GRANITE and other instrusions (various colors, mostly dark)	Unknown	1,000-2,000

THE JOURNEY
ENTRANCE

—

MY JOURNEY began at Hualpai Hilltop, at sunset.
It began in wind and dust and emptiness.

It is always lurking there, this emptiness, at the
threshold of a journey that will start something. And
if it succeeds in breaching an unoccupied moment it
seems to encircle you with a huge, transparent plastic
balloon. Once it has trapped you, the balloon cuts off
the round reality of the outside world. It smothers the
warm reality of emotion. Most certainly of all, it oblit-
erates your ambitions, cancels the very reasons for
your journey. You know that before long you will once
more feel and understand and hope. But at the time
there is only the emptiness.

The emptiness was already there, gray and blank,
by the time Lorenzo Sinyala, the Havasupai Indian
who had driven me over from Grand Canyon Village,
braked his pickup to a halt at Hualpai Hilltop. And it
grew grayer and blanker when I stepped out onto the
dusty parking area. A wind was scything across the
little bulldozed plateau, whipping up dust clouds and
billowing them out and away beyond a sandstone cliff.
We stood on the edge of the cliff, Lorenzo and I, and

looked down at the gray floor of Hualpai Canyon, a thousand feet below. The sun sank behind the far wall of the canyon and the grayness moved up to muffle everything. On the cliff top, each flurry of wind shrouded us in dust. It was a coarse, sandy dust that stung my bare legs and swirled gritty in my face.

Lorenzo pointed off to the right, showing me where the trail hairpinned down a cleft in the sandstone and joined a sandy wash on the floor of Hualpai Canyon before winding away northward and out of sight. It was nine miles, he said, to Supai, the village he had been born in. And twenty miles to the Inner Gorge of the Colorado. He also said that it was thirty years since he had left Supai, and that he had only been back three times. But although I was listening, his words were mere words. For Lorenzo, like the parking area and the sandstone cliff and the billowing dust, existed only thinly, out in the emptiness.

After a while I went back to the pickup, lifted out my pack, and swung it onto my back. Lorenzo and I shook hands. Then I walked to the edge of the parking area and, heavily conscious of the moment's significance, took my first steps down the trail. The emptiness came with me.

The trail fell steeply. As I walked, dust spurted out from under my boots like jets of water. The dust hung suspended for a moment; then the wind whirled it away. I walked on downward. The trail twisted around an immense rock buttress, cut under an overhang, and swung sharp left.

And then I was no longer walking.

I was standing, alone and cut off and not quite understanding why I had stopped, on a natural rock platform that jutted out over Hualpai Canyon. Rough brown sandstone walled me in, blocking off the wind.

I found myself listening. It was so still that there was nothing to hear but silence.

I did not stay on the platform very long. But when I walked on down the trail the emptiness had gone. My boots still sent dust squirting outward, but it did not matter any more. And when I looked down past plunging rock to the gray gravel floor of Hualpai Canyon, the gravel no longer looked gray, but blue-gray with the softness of evening. For I knew now that I had left behind the man-constructed world. Had already escaped from a world in which the days are consumed by clocks and dollars and traffic and other people. Had crossed over, at the moment I came to the sandstone platform, into a world that was governed by the sun and the wind and the lie of the land. A world in which the things that mattered were the pack on your back and sunlight on rough rock and the look of the way ahead. A world in which you relied, always, on yourself.

By the time I came down onto the floor of Hualpai Canyon it was almost dark, and as soon as the slope had leveled off I walked away from the trail and found a flat, open place on one of the rolling fans of brush-covered gravel.

Even before I had slipped the pack off my back I felt a comforting familiarity about my bedroom. The semi-darkness did not quite hide the cleanness and openness of the desert, which I always forget. And I could sense again its apparent barrenness and actual detail.

Soon I was feeling grateful too for the familiar rewards of simple living—for the cleansingly primitive habits and precautions.

When I began to search with my flashlight for a few of the brittle sticks that pass for firewood in this kind of country I knew that it would be all too easy to lose my pack on that almost featureless gravel fan. So I searched in a straight line, switching off the flashlight from time to time and checking my direction by a distant white blob that still showed faintly in the last, lingering daylight. Coming back, I steered by a silhouetted buttress of canyon wall with a single star already glittering above it. When my pack loomed up again, one shade blacker than the night, I felt a small but distinct sense of achievement.

All evening the pleasurable familiarity persisted. When, needing paper to light a fire, I pulled the toilet roll out of its plastic bag and the movement set flashes of static dancing in the dry air, I felt a childish excitement. And after the fire had flared up—pushing back the darkness and adding, as a campfire always does, a warm and dancing element of cheer—I sat and watched the sparks fly out into the night in their harmless desert way. Watching them, I felt much as you do when you come back at last to a fondly remembered house: somewhere along the line, time has erased the details; but now it is as if you had never been away.

When I began to set up camp by the flickering light of my little fire, I quickly found myself dropping into back-packing routines that I have evolved over the years. In themselves, the acts I performed were trivial and unimportant. But they too signaled simplicity. And I knew that they, or variations of them, would form the daily framework of my journey. Soon that framework would exist almost unnoticed. But now, on this first evening, the freshness of renewed familiarity stamped every act on my conscious mind.

Even before I began searching for firewood, I had from habit propped up the pack with my long bamboo walking staff by angling the staff's butt into the soft gravel and jamming its head under the top crossbar of the aluminum pack frame. Now, with the fire well alight (though needing constant replenishment, for desert firewood burns like forest tinder), I positioned the pack more carefully, up at the head of the little patch of open gravel I had chosen. And I dug the butt of the staff more deeply into the gravel, so that the pack would stand firm even when I used it, as I always do, for a back rest.

Then I undid the flap of the big gray pack bag and took out everything I would need for the night. As usual, I had packed the gear so that the things I expected to need at the next halt would come out in roughly the order I needed them.

First I took out two half-gallon water canteens (there were two more further down) and laid them on the gravel, close beside the pack.

Then I unpacked and immediately put on the light, down-filled jacket that was the only warm upper garment I had brought. The evening was not cold yet, not at all cold. And there was nothing that could quite be called a breeze. But already I could feel—especially where my shirt clung damply to the small of my back—the slight downhill air movement that you so often find at night in desert canyons.

Next I took from the pack a blue coated-nylon poncho that on this trip, when I expected no rain after the first two or three weeks, would have to triple as raincoat, sun awning, and groundsheet. The poncho was brand-new, and tough, and I hoped it would not develop big holes too quickly from being used as a groundsheet. I spread it out flat, in front of the pack, with its left edge about three feet from the fire.

Next I lifted out of the pack the big plastic laundry bag that held all the food I would need for the next twenty-four hours. (The balance of the week's rations was in another big bag, down at the bottom of the pack.) I put the food bag on the groundsheet, on the side nearest the fire. Then I took out my two nesting aluminum pots—old and rather battered friends of many years' cooking—and removed the plastic bag that always wraps them and tucked it in securely between pack frame and pack bag, where no sudden gust of wind could whisk it away during the night and where I would reach for it quite automatically in the morning. Back on Hualpai Hilltop I had emptied into the smaller pot a four-ounce package of diced dehydrated potatoes, half a cup of water, and some salt, so that by dinnertime the potatoes would be rehydrated and would need only about ten minutes of cooking, not half an hour. Now I emptied the vegetables into the big pot and washed the last clinging dice free with water that would be needed anyway for cooking the potatoes.

Next I took my little Svea stove out of the pack, removed the stove from its plastic bag, and tucked this bag too between pack frame and pack bag. Then I inserted the stove handle into its socket, grasped the handle between finger and thumb, and held the stove about a foot above the fire. After a moment or two I set the stove down just beside the groundsheet, twisted it a couple of times to bed it firmly in the gravel, and opened the jet valve a half turn. Liquid gasoline, warmed by the fire, welled up out of the nozzle, ran down the stem, and began to collect in a hollow at its base. When I could see in the bright beam of my flashlight that the hollow was almost full, I closed the valve and put a match to the gasoline. A blue-and-yellow flame enveloped the stem of the stove. Cupping my hands, I shielded it from the air movement. When the flame began to subside, I opened the valve. The stove roared into life. It was good, I found, to hear that familiar roar. Good to hear it once more against the silence of the night. Against the huge, soft, black, familiar silence.

I put the pot with the potatoes and water onto the stove and went back to setting up camp. (This freedom to do other things while food cooks is one reason I rarely cook over a campfire. Other advantages include speed, ease of control, and avoidance of collecting firewood—except when you want a fire for warmth or cheer or both. Also—and this is no fiddle-faddle—a stove does not begrime your pots, and so they never coat hands or clothing or equipment with a layer of soot that is invisible at night but can be an unholy nuisance.)

When I had added a few sticks to the fire and then stepped a couple of paces away from it to take a quick look out into the night (just enough of a look to see that a faint paleness still hung along the high western horizon, up above the wall of the Canyon), I took my hip-length air mattress out of the pack and began to blow it up. I inflated the main section hard and the pillow section soft (the reverse of the way I would want it for sleeping on), so that it would make a comfortable chair when propped against the pack with the pillow downward.

Finally I unrolled my new ultralightweight, down-filled, mummy-type sleeping bag and draped it over the air mattress. Its bright orange nylon shell shone warmly in the flickering firelight.

The firelight also showed, now, clouds of steam billowing out from under the lid of the cooking pot on the stove. I turned the stove dead low. The roar abated; but it still shut off, like a massive studded door, the silence of the night.

I sat down on the mummy bag and took off my boots and put them beside the groundsheet on the side away from the fire. I took off my socks too, and hung them half in and half out of the boots. Then I anointed my feet sparingly with rubbing alcohol from a small plastic bottle, taking great care to keep it well away from the fire. The alcohol felt as delightfully refreshing as a dive into a swimming pool after an August day in the city. As soon as it had dried, I unzippered the mummy bag part way, pushed my feet down into it, pulled the bag up loosely around my waist, and leaned back. It was very comfortable like that, with my butt cushioned on the pillow of the air mattress and my back leaning against the firmly inflated main section, which in its turn leaned against the now almost empty pack. I sat there for several minutes, content, relaxed, drifting—hovering on the brink of daydreams without ever achieving anything quite so active.

It was the smell of boiling potatoes that brought me back to the present. Now, boiling potatoes cannot by any stretch of the imagination be said to give off an ecstatically delightful aroma. But the moment I became conscious of their heavy odor wafting past on the clean desert air I experienced a sudden sharp spasm of pleasure. For the smell set free, like lifted sluice gates, a flood of wilderness memories. All at once I was reliving a hundred dinners cooked in this same pot on this same stove while I leaned back, just as I was leaning now, against air mattress and pack. I found myself remembering warm desert valleys with the sun's afterglow still reddening distant hills, and damp, dark forests with tree trunks flickering mysteriously into and out of an uncertain firelit existence, and cold, invigorating mountaintops on which I cooked and lived and slept and thought far above the petty world of man. These vivid and unexpected memories swept aside the last lingering pockets of the emptiness that had encircled me on Hualpai Hilltop. And suddenly I found myself looking forward with a new and knife-edge eagerness to the two months of simple living that lay ahead.*

I leaned forward and, with a red all-purpose bandana insulating my hand, lifted the lid off the cooking pot. The smell of potatoes enveloped me. I tasted them. They were almost cooked. I crumbled in a bar of pemmican (three ounces of processed meat, fifty per cent protein and fifty per cent fat, said to be the nutritional equivalent of a one-pound steak), added a few flakes of instant onion, and gave the mixture a brief stir. By the time I had added another stick to the fire and with my pocket thermometer had checked the ground temperature well away from the fire (it was 62 degrees), the "stew" was ready.

I half poured, half spooned some of it into my stainless-steel cup, set the pot close beside the fire to keep it warm, and switched off the stove. The soft, black silence of the night surged in once more, surprising me as it always does by the way it underlined how loudly the stove had roared.

I leaned back in my chair and ate dinner, spoonful by spoonful, cupful by cupful. It was pretty plain fare, but although I knew I would have found it extremely

---

*I am always being reastonished at the way our sense of smell can bring memories flooding back. Several months after I came up out of the Canyon—when I was deeply embroiled once more in the complexities of the man-made world—I was checking over some old equipment when I chanced on the blue nylon poncho-groundsheet that I had spread out for the first time that evening in Hualpai Canyon. It was by now anything but brand-new. I lifted it up and saw that it was still tinted red with Grand Canyon dust. And at once I smelled the dust. I can find no adequate way to describe what my nose reported, for when it comes to smells our language is poverty-stricken. But I know that the instant I smelled the dust from that tattered poncho there surged back into my mind the reality of what life in the Canyon had been like. I do not mean just that I remembered specific details. I knew once more, in a flood tide of certainty that invaded all my senses, the forgotten essence—the whole clean, open, sunlit, primitive freedom of it.

unappetizing out in civilization, I was no longer out in civilization, and it tasted good. As I ate, with the stove silent now and the fire burning low, I could once more hear and see the night. It was very quiet, out there in the darkness. The western glow had finally vanished, and the sky was all blackness and stars.

As always, dinner was surprisingly filling, and I only just managed to eat it all. When I had finished, I swabbed off with toilet paper the worst of the stew that still stuck to the cooking pot (there was no water to spare for washing up) and burned the paper in the last embers of the fire. Then I half filled the big cooking pot with water for morning tea, and put four ounces of dehydrated apple-and-date nuggets and a cupful of water into the small pot so that the fruit would be ready for breakfast. I stood up, moved to the foot of my groundsheet, and urinated into the night. After that I let most of the air out of the main section of the air mattress and inflated the pillow section fairly hard and laid the mattress flat on the groundsheet, pillow up near the pack. Then I got back halfway into the sleeping bag and removed from my pockets all the things that might fall out when I took my clothes off or that I might need during the night— pen and pencil, notebook, thermometer, glasses case, flashlight, and so on—and put them in the bedside boots. And then, instead of sliding down into the sleeping bag, as I had intended, I found myself still sitting and looking up and out into the night.

The fire had almost died now, and I could see, high above on either side, the silhouetted canyon walls. They stood wide apart. Up to the right, I could make out the hump of Hualpai Hilltop; could soon picture quite clearly the trail that twisted down through brown sandstone to the platform on which, two hours earlier, I had first moved inside the silence. And I found I could remember—could see almost more vividly than when I stood there—the sweep of the rounded sandstone and the clean, sharp lines of its strata. The strata showed how the rock had been built, layer on layer, by day after year after century of wind-blown dust. By much the same kind of wind as had blown on Hualpai Hilltop that evening, and by much the same kind of sandy dust as had stung my legs and swirled gritty in my face. According to current estimates, the sandstone had been built this way 200 million years before, and I accepted that this was what had happened. Accepted it, I mean, with my intellect. I had read the facts. Had read that the Colorado River, in the seven million years it took to gouge out the Canyon, had laid bare the ages. Had exposed them, layer on eloquent layer, so clearly that even the untrained eye can soon come to understand them. Can understand them intellectually, I mean. But that is all.

The figures are the trouble. For the Canyon has existed for a bare flicker of a nod compared with the rocks that it has exposed. The youngest, up at the Rim, are 200 million years old; the most ancient, deep down, more than one and a half billion. But our human minds at first reject the reality of such time spans. For one thing, we find it hard to grasp their magnitude—partly, perhaps, because we still have to measure them with such pitifully inadequate tools as "years." We can, without too much difficulty, comprehend the century that a very old man has lived. With an effort we can add twenty such life spans together and ease ourselves back into the time of Christ. But for most of us Babylon has already faded halfway to legend. And beyond that we wallow, helplessly.

But the real barrier to understanding is fear.

I can still remember the first time I heard man described as a newcomer on earth. I remember how my young mind fought the humiliating idea, and went on fighting it well beyond childhood. Perhaps the war is still not over. I suspect that most of us let a part of our minds struggle on for a very long time. But the truth, once glimpsed, is always there, gnawing away.

As I sat in my sleeping bag on the floor of Hualpai Canyon, looking up into the night at the silhouetted sandstone and imagining the clean, sharp lines of its strata, I tried to make myself see the wind and dust actually creating the strata two hundred million years before. But even with the catalysis of starlight I could not quite bring the picture into focus. In the end I had to admit that "two hundred million years" did not really mean much to me. I could not visualize such a time span as something that had actually happened. Could not yet accept it in the way I accepted that the old man had lived for almost a century. Not yet.

I slid down into the mummy bag at last and undressed and stuffed the clothes into the pack behind my head. Then I pulled the tapes of the mummy bag halfway (tight enough for warmth, loose enough for me to watch the night); and as I floated gently down and away into the shadowy channel that leads over from wakefulness into sleep—a channel that is so often illuminated by flashes of insight—I glimpsed the problem of the ages from a different angle. I had been worrying, I saw, about the wrong things. In the end, the figures would not be what mattered. They are only the tools.*

---

*The figures change anyway. Even the seven million years that I have said it took the Colorado to create the Canyon represents only a rough average of current expert opinion. Geologists' estimates presently vary from one to twenty-five million years. And tomorrow the bracket may broaden. So if you do not feel comfortable with seven million years or 200 million years or such other figures as I shall use, settle for numbers that satisfy you. As long as they're big enough—too big to make much sense— their accuracy is not, for our purposes, all that important. Not yet, anyway.

RECONNAISSANCE

—

FOR TWO days I moved, very slowly, deeper and deeper into the Canyon. I moved down from Hualpai Canyon into Havasu Canyon. On the third morning I passed through Supai village. And all this time I lived on the surface of things. I accepted the restriction resignedly, for any journey into wilderness involves a curious and stubborn paradox.

You know, of course, that you are going to renounce the complexities of civilization and embrace the simple life. And you know that the simple life can lead to insight: even our brusque Western tradition sometimes admits that it is so. But what you are likely to overlook is that your mutiny means making two separate escapes. Obviously, you have to shake off the myopic thoughtways of our man-centered world. But you discover that the tools you have chosen for the escape—solitude and simplicity—at first build new walls. For the trivia take over. And they screw you tight to the present. You wrestle with blisters and sweat rash and upset stomach, with socks that ruck and clothing that rubs and pack straps that slip and food that persistently burns. You anoint and experiment and adjust and readjust. You worry, all the time, about where the next water is coming from, or the next warmth, or the next shelter. And before long you come to realize that these mundane matters are devouring the days.

A peremptory physical challenge, though it will help in the end, begins by making matters even worse. You are forever checking the map, assessing today's achievements, setting tomorrow's targets. And the rare moments when you have a deep, round thought to contemplate always seem to come just when it is time to push ahead again.

These earthy barriers foil your hopes of a quick and total escape from civilization. Experience may help you to break free more quickly, but that is all. In the end you come to accept as something that has to be faced at the start of every journey the stubborn and inescapable paradox of simple living.

That first stimulating evening on the floor of Hualpai Canyon, when I at least glimpsed the underpinnings of geology, had been a sharp and welcome exception to the paradox. But I knew the general rule. And it had been very much in my mind when I roughed out in advance the probable "shape" of my journey.

First, I had decided, I would spend a week in safe, tourist-visited Havasu Canyon, near Supai village. That week would be part shakedown cruise, part hardening period, part reconnaissance.

Then, provided the weather had been right for rain-pockets, I would climb up out of Supai onto a broad and sparsely watered rock terrace, two thousand feet above the Colorado, known as the Esplanade. For two weeks or more I would strike eastward along the Esplanade and its unnamed extension until I came to

Bass Trail. I knew that all through those two weeks I would be grappling, close and sweaty, with the trivia.

But beyond Bass Trail the challenge would ease. Water would become a rather less critical problem. I would even find old man-made trails. But the chance of meeting men on them seemed remote, and I hoped that as I moved eastward along the Tonto Platform, still a thousand feet above the river, the hours and days and weeks of solitude would begin to tell.

Roughly halfway I would reach the only inhabited place in the Canyon outside Supai village: Phantom Ranch, a small, Park-concession tourist hotel that stands on the floor of the Canyon, midway on the mule and hikers' trail running directly across from Rim to Rim. On the second half of my journey the water problem would become even less pressing. By then, too, my body would be honed. And time would have deepened the solitude. I was not sure what I would find beyond Phantom, or even what I hoped to find (though I was already intrigued by reports of ancient cliff dwellings and by an account of a "fifty-room Indian village," once discovered but now "lost" again). Yet somehow I felt confident that beyond Phantom I would find whatever uncertain grail I was going down into the Canyon to look for.

The first week of my journey, then, had been set aside as a combined shakedown cruise, hardening period, and reconnaissance. It turned out to be a more important week than I had expected.

In those first three days, as I moved down deeper into the Canyon—from Hualpai Canyon into Havasu Canyon, and down through Supai village—I cleared up most of the minor equipment difficulties that plague you at the start of any trip. And I began to work myself into shape.

Of course, you always mean to start a long walking trip in good physical condition. Your plans wisely include a series of lengthening workouts with full pack. But the pressure of last-minute preparation always seems to crowd them out, and you arrive at the starting point not only mentally exhausted but equipped with flaccid muscles and slipper-soft feet. This time I was particularly unready. For two frustrating weeks I had lain fallow in Grand Canyon Village while an infected heel cleared up, and now, with a sixty-pound pack on my back, I had to treat feet and muscles with more than usual care.

But new pressures were already building up. Pressures of time and space and weather. My route along the Esplanade became tolerably safe only when storms had punctuated the rock with rainpockets. But the year's winter storms had been light and scattered, and the spring ones had so far failed to materialize. Until heavy rain fell, the Esplanade would be a hazardous proposition.

My only alternative was the Inner Gorge of the Colorado—that narrow final chasm, two thousand feet deep and almost sheer, through which the river often flows.

No one, it seemed, had ever attempted the Gorge on foot. Boat parties who had run the river all reported that in the twenty vital miles above Havasu Creek, the Canyon was at its most awe-inspiring. On either side, they said, a series of rockwalls plunged two thousand feet down to the river. No man could hope to find a way through on foot. But it occurred to me that an unlandlubberly boatman would have his attention riveted on the perils of the river and not on details along its edge. The one short movie sequence and two old photographs of the Gorge that I had seen supported this gleam of hope: all showed a narrow, steeply sloping ledge at the foot of one or both of the rockwalls. I had a bonus going for me too. The Colorado is the third longest river in the United States, and is muscled accordingly. At least, it used to be. But four weeks before I began my journey it had been emasculated. The gates of the new Glen Canyon Dam, sixty miles upstream of the Park, had been closed. And all the time I was in the Canyon the river would probably flow at about one third or one quarter of its previous normal low-water level. No one seemed to have much idea whether this artificial drought would open up sections of gorge previously thought of as impassable, but I meant to find out. Unless rain or snow fell along the Esplanade I had, in any case, precious little choice.

So, late on the fourth day of my journey I left some heavy gear at my campsite near Supai (because I would be returning to the village within three days to pick up supplies for the following week) and set off down Havasu Canyon for a reconnaissance of the Inner Gorge.

Before the day was over I discovered an obstacle that all my careful planning had overlooked.

For almost three hours below Supai I followed, and often waded, the rushing blue-green waters of Havasu Creek. By the time I heard the roar of Beaver Falls, halfway between Supai and the Colorado, the light was failing. Soon I came to a bluff that stretched across the narrow canyon, creating the falls. And at its edge the trail I had been following stopped. Just cut off, dead. It was rather like starting across a high bridge and finding yourself on the brink of a missing span. The bluff dropped away sheer: fifty feet of rough red travertine rock—a limestone coating deposited on the bedrock by the heavily mineralized waters of the creek. In the gathering gloom I could see no way around this bluff. And on either side, little more than a hundred yards apart, towered the huge Redwall cliffs that form the walls of Havasu Canyon.*

Standing there irresolute at the abrupt end of the trail I found myself, for the first time since leaving Supai, really looking at the cliffs. Evening had already stolen their color, and they were two soaring, impenetrable blanks. Their rims, almost a thousand feet above me, ran black and stark. The strip of pale sky between them looked very narrow. Until that moment I had not realized how far I had come down into the earth.

Pushing uneasiness aside, I cast about for a way around the bluff. In the half-light I could find no hint of one. And after a while I accepted that there was nothing to do but camp.

Somehow, it seemed a somber decision. I knew, of course, that this was no real check: in daylight the trail would show. But I stood for a moment in the half-darkness, hesitating. The strip of sky between the Redwall cliffs was very pale now, almost ready for the stars. The rims looked an immense distance away. And when I began to hunt for a campsite among the jumbled rocks I found myself still acutely aware of the depth of the black chasm in which I would sleep. The monotonous, booming roar of Beaver Falls seemed to mock my frailty.

I camped in the only level place I could find, where the trail zigzagged between two blocks of travertine. As I unrolled my sleeping bag it occurred to me that I had chosen a perfect place for a bobcat or mountain

---

*The Redwall is a sheer red cliff, a fairly consistent six hundred feet high, that stands about halfway between Rim and Gorge and seems from the Rim to hold together the fabric of the Canyon's layered master pattern. The rock that forms the Redwall is, oddly enough, blue-gray. Blue-gray limestone. But rain seeping down from the iron-bearing rocks above has everywhere stained its surface a rich and beautiful red.

lion to turn one of the trail's blind corners and stumble on my helpless, cocooned figure. I could picture the animal startled into panic and changing from the timorous and retiring creature that it normally was into a snarling, clawing menace. Wondering a little at my sudden timidity, I laid warning blocks across the trail: on the downwind side, a few sticks of the firewood I had already collected; on the upwind side, a coil of nylon rope that would hold my scent. Afterward, I felt better.

Before cooking dinner I rested for a few minutes, stretched out on my sleeping bag. And it was then, lying on my back and watching the first stars glimmer their hesitant way into that pale strip of sky, lying there with the roar of Beaver Falls filling the night around me, that I felt the weight and power of the Redwall.

A few weeks earlier I had read John Wesley Powell's account of how the boat party he led downriver in 1869 forced what was almost certainly the first passage ever made of Grand Canyon. And I had wondered at the oppression that reverberated through the journal's pages: Powell, a tough, one-armed Civil War major, was obviously not the timorous type. But now, lying on my back at the bottom of the black Redwall gorge, I understood. I was hopelessly insignificant. Insignificant and helpless. A mere insect. And when we humans feel this way we are, inevitably, afraid.

Out in the world you may, very occasionally, look down at night from a high and lonely vantage point onto the swarming life of a great city and catch a frightening glimpse of your own personal insignificance. But that is not quite the same thing. You do not feel, achingly, the utter insignificance of all mankind, and you therefore escape the sense of final, absolute, overwhelming helplessness.

Beneath the Redwall at Beaver Falls, the helplessness lasted only a few minutes. But while it was on
me I recognized, deep down and naked, that before I
could master the Canyon's physical challenge I must
face, sooner or later, a trial of the spirit.

I sat up and lit my cooking stove. Its roar drowned
the roar of the falls. Soon I had a fire going too. It
injected life and warmth into the red travertine blocks
that were my room. It set shadows dancing behind the
room's ornaments: a slender green bush and a prickly
pear set at just the right angle. And it thrust away the
night. But when I lay back on my sleeping bag, waiting for dinner to cook, there was still, far above, only
a starry sliver of night sky clamped between the two
walls of towering and terrible blackness. And there
was still, deep down, the lingering knowledge of my
utter insignificance.

Next morning, in daylight, the Redwall once more
looked red and friendly. I found the trail around
Beaver Falls without difficulty, and hurried on down
beside Havasu Creek.

Ever since Hualpai Hilltop I had been acutely
aware of how much hinged on my Inner Gorge reconnaissance; and when, a couple of hours below Beaver
Falls, I saw the far rockwall of the Gorge looming up
ahead, I found myself suddenly nervous.

My first glimpse of the Colorado was a moderate
relief. The river was big, but not hopelessly big. If
anything, it looked narrower and less turbulent than
I had dared hope. Less intimidating, certainly, than
the huge waterway, three hundred miles downriver,
that I had come to know on another long foot journey—and had come to respect.

But after the relief came doubt. Not the kind of doubt you can define and exorcise, but a vague and elusive sense of insecurity.

A raw wind was gusting up the Gorge. It brushed ugly patterns across the river's surface. The river was a somber, muddy brown, and the dark rock that imprisoned it, pressing in from either side, was lined and ancient, portentous with age. High above the first cliffs, set back only a little, rose the Redwall. It did not look very big now. And above it towered other cliffs. The rims of the Gorge, more than two thousand feet above the river, thrust jagged buttresses against gray and threatening cloud banks. Compared with this gloomy chasm, the Redwall gorge of the night before seemed an almost friendly place. Here even the silence was somber. The roar of rapids only deepened it.

But as soon as I had grasped the new, huge size of things I was gratefully surprised to find that everything looked much as it had in an old photograph of this place that I had seen. It was oddly comforting to pick out a familiar triangle of sand at the foot of a cleft, and a flat rock platform just above the point at which the muddy Colorado began to snuff out the blue-green waters of Havasu Creek. Best of all, when I came down to the river's edge and looked upstream I saw, exactly as the photograph had shown it, a narrow shelf that ran along beside the river at the foot of the first cliff. A jutting outcrop of solid rock hid the beginnings of the shelf, but it looked from a distance as if a man should be able to make his way along it.

I slipped off my pack, unclipped the thermometer from my shirt pocket, and held it in the river. The water felt quite warm. And that was another relief. The rockshelf almost certainly did not extend unbroken along any one side of the Gorge, so I would probably have to cross the river several times. While this prospect would never exactly enthrall me, I knew that the river's temperature could make a critical difference. You cannot swim far in liquid ice, cannot even live in it for very long; but your body will work efficiently for quite a long time in 50-degree water. Because of the new Glen Canyon Dam, no one seemed to know quite how cold the Colorado would be running now; generally speaking, dams tend to lower a river's temperature. After about a minute I took the thermometer out of the water. It read exactly 60 degrees.

Almost cheerfully, I undressed and put on swimming trunks (tourists visiting Supai occasionally came down to this place). Even out of the wind, the air was two degrees colder than the river. I waded Havasu Creek and with wet, bare feet climbed carefully along the jutting outcrop that hid the shelf. Centuries of racing water had polished the black rock to a slippery glaze. But the water had cut fluted depressions, and the inlaid pattern—like a mosaic of black, empty, upturned mussel shells—gave my toes a tenuous, welcome purchase.*

As I traversed along the rockledge, gusts of wind whipped rawly across my skin, sucking away the warmth like a vacuum cleaner. I reached the apex of the jutting outcrop. And at once I forgot the wind. For in front of me the ledge tapered off sharply, then vanished. And beyond it a cliff sliced down and away in a savage, unclimbable overhang.

I found myself looking out beyond the overhang. The way along the shelf, the route that would mean success or failure, looked even easier now. And at its near end a sandy beach sloped gently up from the wa-

---

*I have since been told that, objectively, this limestone formation is dark gray. But I know that on that sullen day, in the mood I was in, it was a funereal and undeniable black.

ter's edge. But between this beach and me, like a protecting moat, stretched a broad back eddy of the river.

Barely one hundred and fifty feet separated me from the beach and the vital shelf. But I could tell that close against the rock the water was deep. Very deep. Except when the wind daubed on its ugly brush marks, I could see steady upstream movement. Once or twice, swirls broke the surface.

Standing there on the rockledge, already shivering, I knew, and wished I did not know, that a hundred and fifty feet of slow-moving water is to most people no kind of challenge at all. But the thought of swimming more than a few strokes has always alarmed me. The act has never pushed me over the brink of panic; but the threat is always there. Even in calm water, nervousness contracts my muscles and quickly and quite unnecessarily tires them. A hundred and fifty feet was probably close to my unaided limit—and I had always swum in open, sunny, populated places, and never with a heavy pack. The one man who had known anything about hiking deep in the Canyon had told me how even at high water he dog-paddled across the river on an air mattress with his pack slung over one shoulder, half-floating. But he was, his wife had said, "like a seal in the water." As I stood shivering on the black rockledge I knew, miserably, that I was no seal. And I knew that in the Gorge, on such a somber day, there was a lot more to it than that.

I waded back across Havasu Creek and dressed and heated some soup on my little stove. After lunch I sat in the lee of a rock and watched the sullen gray clouds, far overhead. Then I dozed. But when I woke up the wind was still there, and the silence, and the roar of the rapids.

It was four thirty before I made up my mind. All along, there had been only one thing to do; now, with less than three hours of daylight left, I could not put it off any longer. I collected together the few things I would need: air mattress, patching kit, poncho, binoculars, waterproof matchsafe, washcloth, nylon cord, and a large sheet of stout white plastic brought along for just this moment. I took off my warm clothes and boots and socks so that I was wearing only shorts, underpants, and shirt. Then I picked up the boots and socks and the little pile of things I would need and walked away from the comforting reassurance of my pack. I waded Havasu Creek again, climbed carefully along the black rockledge, and once more came face to face with the back eddy.

It looked faster now: easier to drift with, but harder to come back against. I knew that if the back eddy defeated me on the way back, I would have to float down in the main current; and now the current looked much farther out, twice as turbulent, and more perilously and inevitably directed toward the roaring downstream rapids. The gray cloud banks, far overhead, had grown even more sullen. The gusts of wind came more often; harder, colder, crueller.

I blew up the air mattress, taking great care not to inflate it too hard because I would need a deep V to lie across. I suspect that I did everything with great care at least in part because I was still stringing out every act as far as it would go. I bundled up all my gear in the poncho—clothes, boots, binoculars, and the rest—and wrapped the white plastic sheet around the poncho and then lashed the plastic sheet tight with the nylon cord. By the time I began to knot the nylon, my hands were shivering so violently that the job took even longer than I wanted it to. I think I told myself that it was only the cold making me shiver.

At last I was ready. There was a moment when, with the white bundle in my hands, I hesitated. Then, reluctantly, as if trying it committed me, I lowered the bundle onto the water. It floated, cocked high. I took it out, balanced it on a little level platform of the black rock, and put the air mattress in the river. It was too limp. The hot breath inside had cooled and contracted. I blew it up harder and put it back in the water. This time it looked about right.

There were no more excuses left now. I took a deep breath, then slid down into the river beside the little green air mattress. It did not really feel warmer underwater than out in the air, but it was a relief to escape the wind.

Keeping close to the rock, very close, I pulled the mattress under me until I was lying with my chest across it. The V was just right, and I felt reassured and surprisingly comfortable. Then I looked up at the white bundle. And at once I saw that there was no room to put it on the mattress, as I had intended.

For what seemed a very long time I just lay in the water, looking up at the white bundle on the black rock and thinking that now I would have to abandon the reconnaissance. As I lay there I noticed that water running down from the bundle had turned the black rock even blacker. It seemed an interesting fact. All this time, inevitably, my determination was seeping slowly away. But then, almost as if I were hovering above the water watching my own antics, I saw that all I was doing was continuing to make ridiculous excuses. And then, leaving no time for second thoughts, I had grabbed the bundle and stuffed it under my chest and pushed off.

Over the brink, everything was easier. Very slowly, the back eddy began to carry me upstream. There were cracks in the rock just above water level, and I slipped the fingers of my right hand into them and pulled. Every time I pulled, the rock moved smoothly past. Nothing else existed now except the black rock and the brown river and my little green air mattress. And the river was only a few inches of water between mattress and rock.

All at once, just when there were no cracks for my fingers, a swirl began to carry me out and away. The few inches of water widened to a foot, to three feet, to four. I found myself kicking with suddenly tensed legs, dog-paddling with desperately cupped hands. For a moment I went on moving out into the river. The rapids were suddenly very loud. Then, slowly, I came back to the rock.

Pulling with fingers and kicking with feet, I began to move along with the back eddy again. Soon there were no more cracks in the rock, only the black mussel-mosaic; but the river was still carrying me forward. And then I was under the overhang and the rock had slanted back and left me out on my own. Immediately, the river was very big. And back in the gloom at the base of the overhang, water lapped quietly against black rock.

I was past the swirls now, in quiet water that no longer helped me forward. I began to dog-paddle. As I paddled I kept looking ahead at the beach that sloped up to the shelf. It did not seem to get any closer. The mattress, reassuring though it was, made the dog-paddling hard work, and my muscles began to contract again. Then, almost unexpectedly, the beach looked closer. And then much closer. By the time I let my legs sink and felt toes touch sand, my muscles felt almost relaxed.

Coming up out of the water—clambering up the steep and yielding sand with the white bundle dripping in my arms—was like coming up out of a pit into sunlight. And when I dropped everything and began to dance around on the sand like a dervish I wondered, even while I was dancing, whether the dance was mostly to get warm or mostly to release the great flood of elation that would not stay down.

In the water I had hardly noticed the cold. But now the wind was cruel again on my wet body. As soon as the elation would let me, I stopped dancing and unwrapped the white bundle. Everything was bone dry. I toweled briefly with the washcloth, pulled on my clothes, and ducked thankfully into the poncho, out of the wind. And then I had grabbed the plastic sheet and the air mattress and, with water still dripping from them, was running full tilt up the sloping beach. The first strides brought a promise of real warmth.

The sand ended and the shelf began. The shelf was a sloping layer of small rockledges, each so narrow that at times it would not accept a boot; but all the ledges angled inward, so that even where they had crumbled your feet could not slip. And each time I came to a doubtful place the ledges were still there.

Right from the start I traveled fast. Even with a heavy pack I could have kept moving. The elation, which had started to go the way of wonderful but fragile things, began to bubble up again.

Half an hour later, I had gone what I judged from the map must be almost a mile. Ahead, the shelf curved on and around and out of sight, unchanged. There was another shelf on the far side of the river. And the river did not look too fast. Not impossible for a timid swimmer with an air mattress who could bring himself to try it.

I would have liked to go farther—at least around the first big bend. But on such a gloomy evening, deep in that somber place, it would be dark in less than two hours. And on the way back it might take longer to cross the back eddy.

I sat down and tightened my bootlaces and marshaled my thoughts. But I knew that I did not really have to think. The decision had made itself. Had made itself while I was moving, unchecked, along the shelf.

There could be no certainty, of course, about the vital thirty miles ahead. But in half an hour I had come almost a mile. Obviously, the remaining twenty-nine were worth a try.

I took a last look upriver, saw nothing to dissuade me, and started back along the shelf.

Now that I knew the way, there was time for me to see more than the next step ahead, and as I hurried along I noticed that the threatening gray clouds had dropped down over the rim of the Gorge. Soon it began to rain. A few big drops at first, unsure of what they wanted to do. Then a couple of flurries, press-ganged by the wind. And then at last, after two false starts, a steady, driving attack. The rain fell noise-lessly on the brown river and noiselessly on the black rock. Its drumming on the hood of my tight-wrapped poncho only deepened the silence outside. I hurried on. The gloom thickened. Once I found myself stopping to listen. All I could hear was the quiet, indifferent lapping of the Colorado.

I had time now to see that all the rock—the black rock around me and the brown rock above it—was cracked and fissured and waiting. Every poised boulder and every peeling fragment hung imminent. I felt that they must all, any moment now, come crashing down on me. It took tight, determined thinking to convince myself that this was not really so.

As I hurried on downstream through the rain I remembered John Wesley Powell's account of his pioneer passage; remembered the oppression reverberating through its pages. And I understood at last—and knew that under the Redwall at Beaver Falls

I had not really understood after all—what the Gorge had done to him, and why three of his companions had finally left him and taken their chance up a side-canyon in a bid for the sky and freedom. (All three reached the Rim; but just beyond it they were murdered—by either Indians or whites.) Now, deep in the Gorge, I found their choice easy to understand. And as I hurried on with the rain still falling silently through the gloom, I knew that in attempting a passage of the Gorge I would face more than a physical challenge.

It was almost a relief to tackle the back eddy again. There was a moment when the current threatened to defeat me. But then, so that I could dog-paddle more freely, I had wrapped an end of the nylon cord around my arm and was towing the white bundle along behind. And soon I was pulling myself up, relaxed again, onto the black mussel-mosaic of the rockledge. Then I was unwrapping the white bundle and thinking, because my icy fingers could not feel anything in the shorts pockets, that I had lost my washcloth. I was shivering so viciously now, with the rain suddenly over and the wind in command, that all the time I was dressing I kept worrying that I might shake my feet off the wet, smooth rock.

The cold no longer mattered, though. I knew it would pass. But when I looked back up into the silent and somber Gorge, I saw that although the gloom had by now grown deeper, the evening was no longer gloomy; and I knew that merely because I had crossed the back eddy and then had returned, the Gorge would never again seem quite such a terrible place. And I knew that this new response would last.

I climbed along the rockledge, waded Havasu Creek, and came home to my pack. And then at last I was pulling on long whipcord pants and down-filled jacket and waiting for the wonderful warmth to spread to hands and feet.

Almost at once, something made me look up. The clouds had lifted. I could see the rim of the Gorge again. And then, far overhead, the clouds moved apart. Through the gap slanted a shaft of evening sunlight. Just for a minute, or perhaps two minutes, a shining cliff face floated high above the far rim of the Gorge, so bright and clear that I could pick out every detail. But the detail was not ordinary rock detail. The outlines of the cliff had been softened by a thin, uneven coating of white.

Before the clouds closed in again I had checked my map. And then I knew for sure. The white cliff stood opposite the Esplanade. And if snow had fallen along the Esplanade there was only one thing to do.

For a time I just stood beside my pack, looking up at the gray cloud banks and hoping for another glimpse of that shining and beautiful cliff. I know I smiled to myself at the way the Gorge had made me forget, until I saw the snow, what rain would mean up on the Esplanade. But I do not think my mind had quite grasped the new shape of things.

Suddenly I realized that the daylight had almost gone. I still had to spend a night in the Gorge. Then, in the morning, I could start doing what had to be done.

I found a good campsite under an overhang. Soon it was dark, and raining again. I lit a fire with sticks I had gathered just before the rain began. The fire's flickering light transformed the overhang into a cheerful little room. With beans bubbling on the stove I sat back in my sleeping bag, leaning against the pack, waiting. My body was glowing now, and tingling; my mind, glowing and content. It had grasped the new shape of things at last, and I could let myself admit, slowly, the relief I felt because I would probably not need, after all, to face a passage of the Gorge.

But I knew the day had not been wasted. Anything but wasted. It had been a great and wonderful and victorious day. A day to remember. And after a while, as I sat there with the stove roaring and firelight playing red on rock and rain falling silvery in the darkness outside, I understood what the day had meant. It had been, I saw, the vital day. The Gorge no longer seemed a terrible place. And because of that the Canyon would no longer hold for me the worst fear of all—the fear of the unknown. I had faced my trial of the spirit.

INTERLUDE

—

THE HAVASUPAI tribe of Indians ("The People of the Blue-Green Waters") live halfway between the Rim and the Inner Gorge of Grand Canyon, halfway between today and yesterday. Their only real links with the outside world are the trail to Hualpai Hilltop and one telephone.

It was to this telephone that I hurried when I got back to the village the day after my Inner Gorge reconnaissance.

"Sorry, line's dead," said the cheerful young tribal tourist manager. "Every time it rains or snows real heavy, water gets into a fuse box up on the Rim. But she'll likely dry out by morning."

And all I could do was wait.

At first I felt frustrated at being unable to telephone Park Headquarters to confirm from weather reports that the Esplanade now looked like a safe route and then to tie up final airdrop arrangements. But before long I saw that the delay was giving me an unexpected chance to look more closely at a unique Canyon exhibit. So I half-stifled my impatience. It was only much later that I realized how the brief interlude in Supai fitted, in its own way, into the pattern of my journey.

Supai is an island in time. On my way down to the Inner Gorge I had been too preoccupied with my own immediate problems of time and space and weather and water to recognize this simple fact. But now that I paused to look around me it was obvious enough, even though I was still too near the start of my journey and too bound up with trivia to look far beneath the surface of things. It should have been obvious, I suppose, before I started. People kept telling me: "Oh yes, the Supai have got a real Shangri-La down there."

My first glimpse had corroborated. It was early morning, my second day below Hualpai Hilltop. I was walking in the shadow of a huge cliff, admiring the grandeur that had opened up a mile earlier when I emerged from the dark inner chasm of Hualpai Canyon into the broad and sunlit spaciousness of Havasu Canyon. And then, at the top of a short rise, I stopped. Beyond the dust and gray rock of the trail, framed by tree-tracery, a lake of foliage floated on pale pink soil. The foliage was green and cool. High above it, hanging red terraces curved vivid in the morning sunlight. Everything sparkled with the magic that makes April the month for seeing new places.

Almost at once there was movement on the trail ahead. First, like eager outriders, two dogs. Then three Indians on horseback: an elderly man who wore steel-rimmed glasses and looked like a sympathetic country doctor; an ample woman in a peacock-blue dress, straining with the effort of leaning forward as her horse climbed the rise, but still managing to laugh down at the two small children she clasped against her body with a free arm; finally, an even more ample man, a beaming avocado of a figure, whose heroic horse barely had room on its back for the child perched in front of him.

My face must have shown what I saw ahead, out in the sunshine, for the avocado man opened up into an even more beamish smile and nodded down at me and murmured: "Good country, huh?" Then he and his companions had passed on up the trail and out of sight.

I walked down the hill into the sunshine. Now there were rooftops scattered among the trees. A horse rolled on its back, kicking delighted hooves. Two very small children erupted from an ancient and sagging beehive of a mud hut, the boy gray-shirted and blue-jeaned and laughing, the pursuing female pink-dressed and determined. They stopped, posed in a tableau beside the dying building, and gravely discussed their crisis of the minute. High above them towered Supai's intricately sculptured backdrop. Off to one side, a deep niche bit down through the red terraces. Almost filling this niche, silhouetted on its own huge, natural knob of a pedestal, stood a massive upthrust of rock. It was shaped like a Grecian urn, beautiful and true, and it was all the tableau needed.

The children wandered back into the blackness of the hut, and I walked on through the sunshine. I walked between two fences now. Beyond each fence, green trees grew in the little pink fields. Irrigation ditches nurtured them. And the houses did not huddle together, as city houses do. From many of them, I was sure, you could see only greenery and red cliffs and blue sky, never your neighbors. But between the fences the trail sulked deep in tourist-trampled dust.

Off the trail, the scene remained idyllic. The only place you could feel you were passing through a village of three hundred people was in the "business center," where three buildings had coagulated. I did my brief business there, then walked on down the trail.

Just beyond the village I came to a little hollow beside Havasu Creek. I slipped off my pack and rested. The creek was warm and unbelievably blue-green, and it sparkled and swirled over tremulous, emerald-green weed beds. Inquisitive little fish nibbled at my inquisitive fingers. Turquoise male damsel flies and their sober brown mistresses made passionate love. White tufts of cottonwood seed drifted on the breeze. And always, high above the green foliage, soared sculptured, buttressed rock cathedrals.

I went on down the creek and came to the first of Supai's waterfalls.

There are three falls, each higher than the last. Each plunges over a wall of red-brown travertine rock that the mineralized water has created in its own image. Overlapping layers of huge, curving stalactites hang pendulous over their own precipice. They are flowing motion, arrested in time. Beneath the seething cauldron of each fall, the mineral of the creek has built little clusters of rock basins. Their submerged walls have not oxidized into the rich red-brown of the precipices. They are porcelain white. And they cry out to be swum in.

Each waterfall, taken as a single work, is superb. The three together overwhelm you.

But even before I went down on my Inner Gorge reconnaissance, the enchantment of the Land of Blue-Green Waters had begun to fade.

First came brutal physical realities. The travertine of the porcelain-white swimming pools cut my feet. The mineralized blue-green waters flaked my skin. Down in the tourist campground everything was quiet, but I knew that the recent Easter week end had attracted a record seven hundred visitors. "They stirred up so much dust," a Park ranger had told me, "that they were like ghosts walking through a mist." Their testimony remained. Dust had spread outward from the trails and laid a gritty, funereal pall over everything; over bedrock and flowers, over cacti and shrubs, even over the foliage of the trees.

When I came back from my Gorge reconnaissance and began waiting for the telephone to dry out, I found that under close inspection Supai's charm wore painfully thin. Everything was dirty and scraggy; dogs, houses, clothing. The tiny pink-dressed child who had erupted from the mud hut, pursuing her male, turned out to have a scabrous forehead. The horse that had rolled in the dust, kicking delighted heels, was rolling, I discovered, to ease a running sore on its back. And the lethargy of lotus land lay over Supai.

This lethargy is modern.

The Supai, as the Havasupai are usually called, must once have been a tough little band to subsist unaided on what the Canyon provided. In springtime they used to forage out many days' journey along the Esplanade to collect agaves, or century plants, and cook huge mounds of them in stone-built "mescal pits." It is said that in winter, when storms create many rainpockets but also make the Esplanade a pretty inhospitable place, the whole tribe used to move up there for hunting.

This Spartan but peaceful way of life probably went on unchanged for six or seven centuries. (The tribe seems to have arrived in what is now northern Arizona some time during the twelfth century.) But at last, as happens in the end to every isolated community, events took an unexpected turn. The white man came to the West.

Because of its isolation, Supai had been able to adjust very gradually to the white man's coming. But once new ideas had reached the Canyon's Rim there began the slow but inevitable adjustment to change.

When a simple-living people discover, ready-made, the tools that another culture has evolved to make life easier, something usually goes wrong; they fail to discover the new goals that these tools demand. The Supai seem to have succumbed to this hazard. It is not difficult to imagine what happened. Once food became obtainable from beyond the trail that led to Hualpai Hilltop, their big family expeditions along the Esplanade ceased. Soon even the men no longer went there. The tribe hunkered down in its lush little oasis. Stagnation set in.

When I inquired in Supai about the Esplanade, even the oldest man in the village had nothing to offer—not so much as a hint about the "little horses" that were still supposed to roam there. He could just remember, he said, being taken out a full day's journey as a young boy and seeing "a big white rock like a monument." When he heard where I intended to go, he cackled: "All alone? But you'll die! No water up in that country, you know. No food, either. You'll die up there, I tell you." And the fat youths who had been lounging around in their fancy but filthy shirts and their black cowboy hats smirked and went on lounging.

I found it sad, after that, to remember the map names along the Esplanade, in what was once Supai country. The first promontory I would pass was called Ukwalla Point. The cheerful young tourist manager was called Neil Ukwalla; but when I asked him about the Esplanade he said that the closest he had been to it was one day when he climbed a thousand feet up a sidecanyon that runs directly out of the village. He had walked half a mile along the narrow terrace that eventually, a day's journey farther on, widens out into the Esplanade. Then he had come back down the next sidecanyon. He seemed to feel that it had been quite an adventure.

The map also showed, at the very beginning of the Esplanade, rising sheer for a thousand feet above the surrounding mesa (or flat tableland), what would almost certainly be the "big white rock like a monument." It was called Mount Sinyala, or Sinyala Butte (a butte is an isolated, steep-sided hill, usually flat-topped). The amiable man who had for twenty dollars driven me from Grand Canyon Village to Hualpai Hilltop in his pickup had been called Lorenzo Sinyala. And I remembered how, in the gray emptiness on Hualpai Hilltop, Lorenzo had told me that in the thirty years since he left Supai he had been back down to the village only three times. He worked all year in the stables at the Grand Canyon Village and owned a new pickup that he kept in good condition and drove very well. And although it had nothing to do with Supai (or perhaps, come to think of it, it did), there was a sadness in remembering now that Lorenzo had found it necessary to strip back the inner covering of the driver's door of his pickup so as to make a little cupboard. And every half hour or so he would reach down and pull out a brown paper bag and roll the top down to the waiting neck of a vodka bottle. And afterward he found it necessary to explain with his benign smile that "a man gets thirsty." And then, after a pause, to add: "Good brand, too. Best in the West."

The white man's today has not, of course, fully dawned in Supai. A passive and contented people living in natural isolation will cling for a long time to their peaceful yesterday, sheltered from the teeming problems that keep the rest of us worried and taut and alive. Even in Supai the slow process of change goes on; but it is not always clear which way the arrow points. There is a tractor in the village (it was packed in pieces down Hualpai Trail); but four days after I first saw it in one of the little pink fields, it still languished in the same place, stalled in midfurrow. And although there are no roads below the Rim, your modern Supai seldom walks: the horses the white man introduced have drugged him as effectively as automobiles have drugged the white man. And, as far as I could tell from my brief stay, the village's old meanings have withered. There was one beautifully woven basket, though, that a tourist had bought. Its craftsmanship was saddening, like the spectacle of a fine old ship being towed away to the breaker's yard.

For a long time after white men reached the Canyon, Supai declined. By the end of the last century the population had sunk to below two hundred. Today it is over three hundred, and still rising. The recovery no doubt had many roots; but one of the strongest began to take hold when tourists discovered the village. For tourism has become its economic lifeblood. The three buildings that make up the business center are a store, a tourist hostel, and a long, patioed building that houses both the post office (said to be the last in America served by pack horse) and a room marked "Office of the Bureau of Indian Affairs" that is really the office of Neil Ukwalla, tribal tourist manager. This bare and grubby room is the economic hub of Supai. This is where you find, on Neil Ukwalla's desk, the village telephone. This is where the braves come to squat and watch each dusty tourist buy a fifty-cent camping permit and a dollar photography permit. Or perhaps it is where they come to avoid being photographed as they lounge their days away outside. Here inside, squatting, they somehow hold the upper hand.

This office is where I came on my second morning

in Supai (it was the sixth day of my journey), to discover whether the telephone line had dried out. Neil
Ukwalla was still counting the takings from the tourist influx of the Easter week end. He had been doing
it the day before too. He rubber-banded the bills into
$100-bundles by denominations: ones, fives, tens, and
twenties. And he laid the bundles out in long, waver-
ing rows. The braves watched. After I had telephoned
Park Headquarters and was waiting for a certain
ranger to call back, I watched too. And as I watched
I found myself hoping that the twenty-four-hour interlude in Supai had given me the wrong impression:
that tourism had in fact done no more than put the
tribal economy back on its feet. But then the phone
rang and Neil Ukwalla deserted for a moment his
marshaled ranks of rubber-banded bills.

"Havasupai Tours Enterprise," he announced. He
held a long and amiable conversation with a potential
customer, and just before he put the receiver down
he said: "But if you're coming before mail can reach
here, why don't you bring cash instead of sending a
check? We'll collect it at roadhead. Sometimes, you
know, we run pretty short of cash down here."

And my hope faded quietly away.

Soon the phone rang again. It was Jim Bailey, the
ranger at Park Headquarters who was keeping a
watchdog eye on me.

"An inch of snow up here right now," said Jim.
"We've had the equivalent of thirty-four hundredths
of an inch of rain in the last four days. And the five-
day forecast is 'cool with showers.' You just couldn't
have asked for much more."

So that was that. We fixed the first airdrop for eight
days ahead, at ten o'clock in the morning. And we confirmed both primary and alternate drop sites: a spring
below Great Thumb Mesa; and, in case I found that

in seven days I could travel farther than this spring, a rainpocket at the head of Fossil Bay.

"Well, take care of yourself," said Jim when we had it all settled. "See you from the plane, a week from tomorrow."

CHALLENGE

———

AT EIGHT thirty next morning, when I stepped up out of a sidecanyon onto a rock terrace, thirteen hundred feet above Supai, I knew at once that along the Esplanade I faced no trial of the spirit. Not, at least, a trial by enclosure. For my map showed that this terrace was a preview of the Esplanade; and I had stepped up into a country of space and light. A country that stirred in me, after a week in constricting sidecanyons, the pleasure of open vision. Now I could look far out across flat red rock and watch the long, swift flight of a cloud shadow. And I found that it was a joy and a release to watch one of these shadows dissolve for a moment as it crossed a sidecanyon, then reappear and race onward, diminishing, until it accelerated up a distant talus slope, vaulted a cliff face, and vanished over the Canyon's Rim, five or eight or even ten miles away.

The discovery of this airy and open and quite unexpected world left me feeling surprisingly well informed about what I could expect to find during the week that lay ahead. For I already knew in considerable detail most of the really critical facts.

That I knew anything at all was due almost entirely to one man.

At the very start of my year of waiting I had begun trying to gather information about foot travel through those parts of the Canyon away from the river and the Rim-to-Rim tourist trail. I inquired of park rangers, packers, geologists, and men who had "run" the river several times. But before long it dawned on me that when it came to extensive hiking in remote parts of the Canyon, none of them really knew what he was talking about. So I set about tracking down the experts on foot travel. In the end I discovered that they totaled one: a math professor at Arizona State College in Flagstaff. But Dr. Harvey Butchart, I was relieved to find, knew exactly what he was talking about. He had been learning for seventeen years.

If I had known seventeen years earlier that I would try to walk through the Canyon when I did I would no doubt have arranged for someone with an inquiring and well-trained mind to move immediately to some place close by. Someone like a math professor, say, to move to Arizona State College. I would have arranged for this man to fall under the Canyon's spell. And I would have had him see the Canyon as a natural obstacle course and an irresistible challenge. I would have tempted him down long disused trails. Then out into the wild places. And before long he would decide that one of the things he wanted most in life was to cover, in a series of three- and four-day trips strung out over many years, the entire length of his obstacle course of a National Park. He would mark the route of each trip on a topographic map. Mark it with mathematical care. He would write accurate notes, too, and record in his well-trained mind a mass of trustworthy information that never got into the notes.

When the seventeen years were nearly up I would

no doubt have had this man write an article on the Canyon's trails in *Appalachia* magazine. Then I would have arranged for that particular copy of the magazine to be tucked under the arm of a friend of mine when, a week after I saw the Canyon for the first time, I expressed a guarded interest in the place. And finally, I would have arranged for my mathematical explorer to be so generously motivated that when I revealed my plans he would invite me to be his house guest in Flagstaff so that he could more easily pass on his hard-won information.

As things turned out it did not matter in the least that seventeen years earlier no such unlikely project as walking through Grand Canyon had entered my young head. It had all happened anyway.

Today, Harvey Butchart is a compact, coiled-spring fifty-five—and a happy and devoted schizophrenic. Teaching mathematics is only one of his worlds. At intervals he lives in a quite different reality. His three-year-old grandson, a young man of perception, recently heard someone use the words "Grand Canyon." "Where Grandpa lives?" he asked, just to make sure.

Harvey fed me a stream of accurate information, first by letter, then on the phone, and finally in person.

To my first question—whether it was indeed possible to traverse the Canyon on foot—he did not quite have a definitive answer. But he came close. Over the years, the ink lines he had drawn on the map to represent his short trips from the Rim had consolidated into a tortuous blue snake that ran almost from one end of the Park to the other. Only one gap remained: a four- or five-mile traverse along a narrow hanging terrace below Great Thumb Point, at the far end of the Esplanade. The Havasupai still had a tradition that this stretch was impassable. But Harvey had stood at each end of it and had looked into two of the three precipitous canyon heads that the map suggested were the ultimate barriers. Each curving canyon head was a natural amphitheater, lacking only the flat central arena.

"They're steep, those amphitheaters," Harvey told me. "Very steep. But I'd guess that they're both passable. Still, you can never really tell with these things until you give them a try. And as for that middle one— I guess we'll just have to wait and see."

Harvey confirmed the tentative ideas I had formed about routes. You could usually, he said, find a way along the hanging terraces. But if the one you were following petered out (as quite often happened to the narrowest of them) you could very rarely climb up or down onto the next terrace. From a mile or two away you might see what looked like a gap in the intervening cliff face, with only a few feet of deeply seamed rock separating two terraces. But you were almost certainly in for one of the Canyon's continual surprises. The scale of the sculpture had unhinged your sense of proportion. Close up, you were likely to find it was not "a few feet" but fifty or a hundred. And although the helpful-looking seams did exist, they ran fifteen or twenty feet apart. In between stretched smooth, unclimbable rock. Almost the only place you had a chance of changing levels was where a section of cliff had collapsed and so much rubble had tumbled down that it had buried the next cliff under continuous talus. Such ramps often looked, as one ranger put it, "as though they only need a man's footstep to start the whole place sliding." Actually, the weight of a man, or even of a battalion, is so insignificant compared with the forces of rock and gravity involved that the danger is negligible.

Harvey gave me all this hard-won information, and

much more, quite ungrudgingly. There was only one moment when he seemed to have second thoughts. It happened just after I went to stay with him and his wife, Roma, in Flagstaff, before I drove up to Grand Canyon Village.

"I'm sure you realize," Harvey had said, "that it's one thing to take on the Canyon the way I do, in a series of small bites from the Rim, but quite another to swallow it whole. Frankly, I'm not at all sure I ought to be encouraging you." He hesitated. "One thing that worries me is that you're not really the right build for the desert."

It wasn't only, I knew, that beside his greyhound of a figure I loomed rather bulky. I was undeniably out of condition. In other words, fat. But I also knew that by the end of the week's shakedown cruise I would have fined down appreciably. "Bet you a nickel I make it," I said. "A brand-new nickel that I can mount as a souvenir."

Harvey grinned. "Okay," he said. "I'll just keep hoping you win. Hoping hard."

And I never heard another word of doubt.

From all that Harvey had said, and also from my understanding of the paradox of outdoor living, I felt that I knew just about how the journey would go in the week beyond Supai, the week that would culminate in the airdrop. Above all, I knew that at this early stage of my journey I should not expect to do more than glimpse, at the very most, the things I hoped to find in the end.

My forecast proved all too accurate. Right from the start, the week developed into a heads-down struggle

with the physical and the present. I found little time
to consider the 200-million-year span of a rock's existence or even the decades of an Indian tribe's de-
cline. All week I grappled with the day and the hour
and the minute and at the very end, with slow, tantalizing seconds. The Canyon had its moments, but
they were desperately rare.

Yet when I stepped up out of the sidecanyon above
Supai at the very start of the week and discovered the
openness and the racing cloud shadows, it was without question one of those moments, and I sat quietly
on the lip of the rock terrace for almost half an hour
and watched the cloud shadows and the rock and the
light. I would have liked to sit there much longer. But
I knew that this was no day for sightseeing. It was the
day that Harvey Butchart regarded as the first test of
my ability to tackle the Canyon.

The terrace I sat on twisted northward to Mount
Sinyala and the beginning of the Esplanade; and not
until I had passed Mount Sinyala and reached Sinyala
Canyon would I find water. On the map it did not look
like much of a day's journey. My map measurer,
wheeled sinuously around the many canyon heads
that cut into the terrace, had recorded barely seven
miles.

But that "seven miles" meant next to nothing.

Cross-country on foot, miles are always misleading:
the hours are what count. In the Canyon, miles become virtually meaningless. From start to finish of
my journey I would cover, in a straight line, only
forty-three. The river mileage came to one hundred
and four. When I ran the map measurer from one end
to the other of my proposed route, carefully following
each winding contour, it registered just two hundred.
But I felt sure, and Harvey Butchart agreed, that I

would walk at least four hundred miles as the foot slogs. And there were times when I would be lucky to travel half a mile in an hour.

Harvey had confirmed my doubts about those "seven miles" for the first day's journey out of Supai.

"I went around that way only last year," he said. "And from Sinyala Canyon to Supai was a full day. Even when you're fit it takes eight hours of hard, fast traveling with a thirty-pound pack. A good eight hours. Equal to every step of twenty miles on the flat."

Now, Harvey had a local reputation for prodigious feats of sustained speed (he has been called The Flagstaff Flyer even in print), and I was still by no means fit enough for real Butcharting. Even more to the point was my pack. It now held a full week's food and two gallons of water, and just before I left Supai it had pulled the arm on the store's scale down to sixty-six and a half pounds. I was prepared for quite a day.

It had begun well, though, and as I turned northward along the terrace and settled down to the long, steady grind toward Sinyala Canyon and water I calculated that I had eleven hours of daylight left and only six Butchart-hours of actual walking to go. Even allowing for rests, it seemed a comfortable balance.

The day turned out to be a curious blend of stupidity and satisfaction.

Almost at once I hit a trail, thick with the prints of horses' hooves. And for an hour the trail turned what would have been slow and sweaty scrambling into fast, easy going. One hour, almost one straight-line mile. Ten hours of daylight left, and only five hours to go. I began to relax.

It was then that the stupidities began. Not to mention the mischances.

First I met the horse. It stood fifty yards ahead; motionless; head hanging dejectedly, like a man dozing his woes away after a bad day at the races. It was sway-backed and stark-ribbed but not, to my surprise, particularly small. I suspected it, therefore, of being a Supai stray; but I also knew it that it might be one of the so-called little horses of the Esplanade.*

Stupidly, I decided that there was plenty of time for me to photograph this miserable but intriguing specimen of a horse. I clamped binoculars in front of my camera lens with a flash bracket, and moved in. Any photographer will understand why, by the time the animal finally bolted, a dozen meticulous shots later, my watch showed that almost an hour had passed. Nine left and still five to go.

The trail promptly petered out. Immediately, my first canyon head: a fan of ravines slashing into the terrace. I found myself edging forward over steep and

---

*Lurid rumors about miniature horses in Grand Canyon have flourished for many years. One clutch of stories tells of pigmy horses, "the size of Newfoundland dogs," captured not far from Supai and put on public exhibition in the outer world. The ancestors of these horses were reputed to have been trapped in sidecanyons by landslides. The progeny, down the generations, had been dwarfed by lack of sunlight, shortage of food, and inbreeding. It seems certain that such stories are outright fiction. Some very small horses have indeed been exhibited in sideshows. But the National Park Service in Grand Canyon has definite information that these beasts came from a horse ranch in Mexico and were runt Shetland-pony-type colts. Their exhibitor had bought them from an enterprising individual who seems, for glamour and publicity, to have invented a "canyon of the little horses" in Grand Canyon, complete with landslides and even some kind of Indian legend. If the story were true, incidentally, their captor could be prosecuted by the federal government for stealing horses from government-owned land.

The second set of stories has a basis in fact but suffers from consistent exaggeration. There are indeed wild or semiwild horses out on the Esplanade (the Supai still lay claim to them, and certainly seem to have had some degree of control over them, at least until about twenty-five years ago). In January 1938 an expedition of three National Park Service men and two Havasupai guides penetrated on horseback along the Esplanade. They sighted twenty-seven horses. Some but not all of the animals were undersized. In the unequivocal opinion of the naturalist in the party they were simply underdeveloped wild horses, the normal result of a skinflint environment. The smallest adult caught by the party measured 50 inches at the shoulder and had a girth of 56 inches. Its weight was estimated at 400 pounds. A rather smaller specimen, about eleven years old, said to have been captured by the Havasupai on the Esplanade three years earlier, was measured in Supai village. Its statistics: 48–53–300.

unstable talus, scrambling up and around one house-size boulder, then easing past another's undercut basement. At last, back onto solid rock. But only four hundred yards in the hour. Lunch and a rest. Seven left now, and three or four to go.

An hour's fast walking over solid rock. Then, as I passed a small bush, a violent pain above my left ankle. Half an hour, and the final extraction of a broken twig-end that had driven in beside my shinbone, firm as a pier piling. Another hour, and thousand-foot Mount Sinyala jutting up at last from the flat mesa ahead like a huge molar tooth.

The sight took some of the pressure off, made me forget that I had begun to feel footsore and a little tired. Sinyala Canyon was just around the corner now, perhaps two hours away. And still four hours of daylight left.

Fifteen minutes later I saw a rainpocket. It was no bigger than a good-sized frying pan, but it seemed the final assurance of success.

While I stood looking down at the rainpocket I noticed that the adhesive tape covering the twig puncture on my leg had worked loose. I swung the pack off my back and unzipped a side pocket.

The moment I saw that the first-aid kit was missing, I knew what had happened.

By the time I had made up my mind, had propped pack against walking staff on top of a prominent rise and begun to hurry back southward, another fifteen minutes had slipped away. An hour of fast, packless walking. And there, exactly where I had sat and extracted the twig, lay the little plastic bag with its roll of tape showing through. Another hour, faster, back to the pack. Almost six o'clock. Two left now, and two to go.

As I moved ahead again, beyond the rainpocket, a

heavy cloud bank doused the sun like a candle snuffer. All at once the evening was prematurely cold and daunting. But an hour's determined walking brought the molar silhouette of Mount Sinyala level with my left shoulder. The grayness began to seem less daunting. Only an hour to Sinyala Canyon. With luck, even less.

And then another stupidity. The final canyon head cut deep into the terrace, back to the very foot of the bounding cliffs. But the canyon itself looked very easy to cross, and I chose the direct route. Hidden dropoffs; overhangs; rock faces seven times as high as they had looked. By the time I climbed onto the far rim another half hour had dribbled away.

But at last, with the day almost dead, I came to the slot that was the beginning of Sinyala Canyon. Five minutes later, clambering down the canyon's floor, I glimpsed a string of palenesses ahead. And then my flashlight was shining into water a foot deep.

I camped at once, there beside the biggest rainpocket. Soon I was sitting up in my sleeping bag, shielding stove and dinner from a cold, blustering wind. I felt well satisfied. Although nothing much had happened, it had been a long day for someone still in pulpy shape, and I felt no more than reasonably tired. And now that I had time to look back at the day I saw that the stupidities had helped to make it a success. It was like getting 100 per cent in a driving test that you were stupid enough to take with a hangover. I felt I had passed Harvey Butchart's qualifying exam with something to spare. And that, after all, was what the day had been for.

In spite of Harvey's briefings I had formed no very clear impression of what the Esplanade would be like. It usually happens this way, I think: you wait for the reports of your own eyes and ears and nose and skin before you construct a coherent picture of a place. But in all my planning the one salient fact about the Esplanade had been that it was enclosed by impassable cliffs; and although I had not really stopped to consider the matter, I think I had connected the terrace, vaguely, with words like "constricted" and "shut in" and even "cramped." Crowded map contours, representing the network of sidecanyons that seam it like gaping cracks in a mud flat, had tended to confirm the impression.

But the Esplanade turned out to be a broad and open place. A country of air and light and distance. An even more spacious land than the open rock terrace that had surprised and delighted me about Supai. For now the cloud shadows raced over red rock for ten, twenty, and sometimes thirty miles before they vaulted out of sight over distant cliffs that were the North Rim of the Canyon.

This airy openness of the Esplanade has a quality that is lacking in the openness of an ordinary plain. Your eye passes smoothly across the rock and joins one flat mesa to the next; but your mind remembers the sidecanyons. It remembers their thin fingers that reach out and isolate the mesas, slicing down into the rock for a hundred, five hundred, a thousand feet. Your mind even remembers, from time to time, the Inner Gorge. You find it difficult, though, to grasp the reality. To accept that off to the left—two miles away, or three, or five—your eye passes without recording it across a gap broad enough to contain the Colorado, across an incision more than two thousand feet deep.

But the knowledge is there, somewhere. And it pollinates the Esplanade with hints and possibilities.

You know too that your eye is suffering another illusion. An illusion of space and texture. For the Esplanade is above all a land of textures. Of textures and colors. You live under a smooth blue sky. Raised white clouds scurry across it. Off to the left your world is bounded by fine-grained cliffs, white and far away. Below them curves burlap talus. Then the red rock begins. First, as fine-grained as the cliffs. Then, when distance no longer hides the whole truth, coarsening. And finally, in the last half mile, slashed and fissured and crumbled into a chaos of ledges and clefts and massive boulders. And this final close-up reveals how smoothly the distant textures have lied.

The Esplanade, I decided at last, was an island in reverse. Not land raised above the sea, but space engraved into the land. Yet it remained an open, not a constricted, place. It just existed within the two bounding lines of cliffs, one close above my right shoulder, the other far away across the red rock. And I accepted the limits. I do not think I was yet aware of how completely they had cut off the reality of the outside world. That awareness did not come until later, much later, when I was almost ready to leave the Canyon. At the time I inquired no further than a continual but fluctuating roar that came from the nearby cliffs, as though waterfalls were cascading down their pale walls. At first I found it difficult to believe that such a solid sound was only the wail of wind tearing at stone buttresses.

The Esplanade, then, was a pleasant place. But it remained a stern and insistent challenge. Above all, every hour of every day, there was the water problem.

Harvey had promised only two or three unreliable

seeps and rainpockets before I reached the far end of the Esplanade. But there I would almost certainly find a spring—though even that had gone dry at least once in the past ten summers.

It was this spring, close under Great Thumb Mesa, that I had chosen as the site for my first airdrop; but we had also arranged an alternate site at a deep rainpocket that Harvey Butchart had recently discovered near the head of Fossil Bay. This rainpocket lay a long day-and-a-half's journey beyond Great Thumb Spring. Naturally, I was hoping to take the drop at Fossil Bay. For one thing, I wanted to push as far ahead as possible while the weather was on my side. Pride came into it too: Harvey had seemed convinced that Great Thumb Spring was as far as I could hope to go in a week. And at first there had been another spur, a severely practical one: at Fossil Bay I would be safely past my route's biggest question mark—the four or five miles of unknown country, with its three steep natural amphitheaters, that Harvey had never crossed. But just before I left Supai a verbal message had reached me that Harvey had succeeded in negotiating these amphitheaters. Although I felt some sense of loss—a certain slackening in the challenge— it was a relief to know that if the message had not been garbled, as verbal messages routinely are, my way was clear. I felt pleased, too, for quite a different reason. Without Harvey's help I could never have planned a route. Not with confidence, anyway. And it was only right that he should be the first man through. I think I already knew, in any case, that although I would still be bound tight by the trivia for at least another week, the physical challenge was no longer what mattered.*

---

*Much later, I learned from a mutual friend why Harvey had tackled the amphitheaters just before I did. He apparently felt far from sure that I was either competent or in good enough physical condition to attempt a

But, at least on the surface of my mind, the target for the week remained, quite clearly, one or other of the airdrop sites.

I knew, of course, that everything depended on water. And the water depended on the weather.

"Before you take off from Sinyala Canyon," Harvey had said, "make dead sure there's been enough rain. You could easily get just enough to make you feel safe out on the Esplanade and then run into a spell of hot weather that would dry everything up fast—including you. I can't imagine a neater trap."

By the time I reached Sinyala Canyon at the end of that long day of blended stupidity and satisfaction, seventy-two hours had passed since the rain that fell on the evening of my Gorge reconnaissance, and I felt by no means sure that there was enough water along the Esplanade for safety.

Partly because of this doubt (and partly because the second day out nearly always seems the hardest on feet and muscles), I had planned something close to a rest day. I would do no more than make a leisurely reconnaissance of a long and apparently unexplored rock fault that looked as though it might be a major short cut. But I would also check, very carefully, how much water the storm had left in the Esplanade's smaller rainpockets.

When I woke beside the big rainpocket in Sinyala Canyon, one day out from Supai, the blustering wind of the night before had honed itself a cutting edge. By the time I struck camp, rain was falling. Not heavily, but with malice. And I had hardly climbed up onto the broad, flat terrace that was the beginning of the Esplanade and begun to look for the unexplored rock

---

stretch of precipitous country that might well turn out to be impassable. So, in his quietly concerned way, he did something about it.

fault—with no very great determination—when the raindrops began to shiver themselves into snowflakes.

The flakes never really got a grip on the wet ground, but for long muffled minutes I would walk imprisoned. The pale brown stalk of a century plant might stand out for a moment, erect and tasseled, like a windswept Maypole. Otherwise there was only a small, flat disk of rock around me, and a vague gray-white outer encirclement. Then the squall would pass. And when I looked back westward I could see faintly, as if through a lace curtain, the thrusting molar shape of Mount Sinyala. But soon another gray-white blanket would swoop down and imprison me once more.

After half an hour, one squall seemed to leave the Esplanade unnaturally bright. Now, when I looked westward, Mount Sinyala stood out sharp and clear, like a floodlit castle. Above it, streaks of blue had begun to partition clouds that were no longer leaden. And then, all around me, the sun was flashing celebration signals from a hundred little pools in the red rock.

It was these temporary rainpockets that reminded me of Harvey Butchart's "no neater trap." The biggest of them looked as if they would hold the trap door open for a week. And suddenly I saw that a rest day had become an unforgivable luxury. Although the rock fault might just possibly conceal a short cut, searching for it would most likely do nothing but waste valuable time. I decided, there and then, that while the going was good I would make a break for it along the known Butchart-route that skirted the bounding cliffs of the Esplanade.

It was from that moment of decision—the final taking of the bit between my teeth—that the week's real business began.

All week I made steady progress. Progress in many things.

Most obviously, there was measurable progress in space. It was very simply measured progress. In the first two days, for example, I went exactly three straight-line miles. But the straight line crossed a deep, many-armed monster called Matkatamiba Canyon. And I could not. I spent the whole of those first two days skirting its outstretched fingertips, back at the very base of the cliffs.

The first day, the sixty pounds on my back felt more like a hundred, and by dusk I had barely passed the main head canyon of Matkatamiba. In a straight line (a line that ran almost at right angles to the two-day straight line) I had come just two and a half miles. But the apparently flat Esplanade imposed a consistently serpentine route. Every step was zig or zag: zig along a sidecanyon; zig again for a side-sidecanyon; then zag along its far side to resume the first zig; almost at once, a new zig for a new side-sidecanyon; and then another zig up a side-side-sidecanyon. And the going was almost never level. All day I kept having to cross or to detour laboriously around little tributary gullies that were hardly deeper than suburban living rooms.

The second day, zagging back along the far side of Matkatamiba Canyon, I went almost three straight-line miles. And that brought me to a seep spring near Chikapanagi Point. It was the last water I could be reasonably sure of finding before Great Thumb Spring, and when I walked away from it early on the third morning out of Supai I knew that I had to put a lot of miles behind me before dark. I succeeded. And surprisingly easily. For although I did not know it yet, the worst of the zigging and zagging was past.

Each day, from the moment of my decision to press ahead, I made progress in other things too, apart from space. Most notably, I made progress in my war with the trivia.

It is often difficult to remember, when conditions have radically changed, what occupied your thoughts most at a certain time. A notebook is the surest guide. My notebook shows, quite luminously, what the important things were in those first days across the Esplanade. It makes sparkling reading: "Tea time: wash sox, fill canteens"; and "Wearing long pants all day, so it *must* be cold"; and "Dawn 4:45, ground temp 32°, sox frozen solid (drying on pack). Frost on sleeping bag, but slept only very slightly cold, naked. No wind, and really very pleasant weather"; and next day: "Lunch 1:30: Shade temperature 76°, in sun 102°." Neck and neck with these weighty matters ran the medical reports: "Twig-puncture nerve still stiff, but seems getting better"; and "Don't altogether like feel of deepish blister forming near ball of left foot"; and "Two travertine cuts on right foot now septic"; and even "Chapped inner thighs, partly heritage from lime of Havasu Creek. Try cocoanut oil on one, fly dope on other. Dope better." In these early days, then, I still labored along under the burden of the stubborn and obtrusive paradox of "simple living."

But even in this tight little world of trivia, things were getting better. Each day my muscles responded more readily to the pack's dead weight. "Chapped thighs" and "twig-puncture nerve" grew less painful. Above all, my feet held out—under a growing patchwork of those oddly miraculous adhesive felt pads called Moleskins. The Moleskins, marked forty cents, were the most precious commodity in my pack. One day I found a five-dollar bill I had tucked into their package for use in Supai and forgotten about. But the useless scrap of paper hardly seemed heavy enough, even by my dram-paring standards, to throw away; and there was always the chance it might come in handy for lighting a fire.

It was the same with camping and cooking and the rest of the daily routine. I still did the same things. But I hardly noticed what I was doing. When I propped up my pack at dusk, when I rolled out the blue groundsheet and inflated the little green air mattress, and when I lit the stove and stirred the stew, the physical acts touched little more than the skin of my mind. The rest of me, the part where the answers can begin, was already part way free to wander and observe and record and ruminate.

As the days passed there was progress, too, in what I can only call "confidence."

It may seem ridiculous for an experienced walker to feel ill at ease about routine matters almost every time he starts a major journey. But more is involved than experience. Whether you like it or not, the occasion tells: most people, I think, suffer some degree of stage fright on their first day at a new job. The sidecanyon up and away from Supai had been in a sense the real beginning of my journey, and I had duly suffered stage fright. Within a mile of the village, traveling too fast over rough ground and moving about as nimbly as a no-toed sloth, I twice stumbled and almost sprawled full length. And the rest of that "Butchart test day" to Sinyala Canyon had hardly been a model of efficiency. Then, out on the Esplanade two days later, I left my pack on the lip of a sidecanyon and went down to look for a seep spring that Harvey had reported; and when I climbed back up there was no sign of the pack. For three or four racking minutes, cursing myself for not checking landmarks, I searched among the rock chaos. Then I came around a boulder I had already passed twice—and there, fifteen feet away, stood the pack. But that was about the end of my elementary lapses.

The really critical progress, though, came in route-finding. And it was the route-finding, more than anything else, that at first kept my mind screwed tight to the present.

The Esplanade, for all its flat and open aspect, is a maze. All along it you face a choice of two routes: rock terrace or talus. The rock terraces mean relatively level going, and they often open up into broad boulevards. But they are not only consistently serpentine—as I discovered around Matkatamiba Canyon—they also keep petering out. And then you have to decide whether to climb ten, twenty, or thirty feet up or down onto the next ledge. You base your choice on the look of the ledges on the far side of the subcanyon you are zigging and zagging along. And this raises one of the scale problems that the Canyon is always posing. A rockface that from a distance looks like something you might have to lift your pack over turns out to be high as a house. As compensation, though, a ledge that promises no more than a handhold may be wide enough to drive a bus along.

But at each major canyon head the rockledges vanish. Rubble from the cliffs has spilled down over the bedrock. To cross these steep talus slides in the least horrifying places you have to climb high; and on the far side of the canyon head you find yourself part way up the talus that always skirts the cliff. The first rock terrace may be a hundred feet below. Or two hundred. And because head and legs both kept reminding you of the old adage, "Never lose elevation unnecessarily," you usually decide to stay up on the talus.

The talus is the direct route. For each mile on the

map you only walk about one and a half. But it is slow and sweaty walking. No striding out, now, along flat bedrock. Instead, weave and detour in and out of low, leg-scratching scrub. Strain and pant along loose gravel slopes. Then struggle and grunt across deep-cut gullies. And still, at every big canyon head, the slides.

At each canyon head you look back. If you have kept low, along the sinuous ledges, you can see that the talus route would have cut miles of meandering and saved a good half hour. If, on the other hand, you have come along the talus you can always see quite clearly that the ledge route would have been only a kickshaw longer and would have saved at least an hour in time and a full pint in sweat.

But after two days I had grasped the pattern of this maze, and my route-finding began to improve. Along the ledges I found myself picking the right levels more often, then holding them more accurately across talus overspills. In time, I realized that the spiky leaves of century plants, which tended to grow about three feet tall, provided a rough-and-ready scale for judging the height of distant rockfaces. And along the talus I began to strike the right line: neither so high that every yard was a scramble nor so low that every gully had dug itself into a gorge. I knew I was doing better because I found myself, more and more often, following faint game trails. For the first two and a half days "game trail" meant only vague indications that several deer had been that way; but at least it was comforting to find myself following in the experts' footsteps.

And then, about noon on the third day, revolution.

All morning the going had been as rough and slow as ever. I had covered barely a third of the final, vital leg to Great Thumb Spring. Then, quite suddenly, I was walking along a trail. A clear, well-traveled horse trail.

This time the trail did not peter out. It intensified. It ran high on the talus, not twisting and turning too tortuously, and along its well-beaten surface I could stride out as fast as along bedrock. And now I could leave the route-finding to the horses.

The difference was critical. It was like driving mile after mile across a strange city on back streets studded with stop signs and then hitting a six-lane boulevard with synchronized traffic lights.

When I looked back later I could see that hitting the horse trail was the turning point. Was the beginning of the end of the paradox of simple living.

But I must not mislead you into believing that even in those first three days of earthbound effort I was totally imprisoned by the brutal immediacies of the physical world. The Canyon, as I have said, had its moments. Deep in a sidecanyon, a Sphinx overhang, massive with hints of wisdom, brooded above a seep spring. A torch cactus, angling out from its crevice, cocked a slyly humorous snook. I lay on naked rock, sipping nectar that an hour earlier had been snow, and all around me the sun distilled voluptuous scents. A whiskered ground squirrel bounced onto a rock, froze, blurred, and was gone. Beyond shadow that still belonged to the night, a day's incoming sunlight streamed across the rock reefs. Noon pressed down onto the Esplanade, hotter each day, more ponderously silent. Evening came, and a softer, richer silence.

Such moments held the promise of progress. Of real progress. Of progress in my pilgrimage. But they never lasted long.

Then, late on the evening of the third day, as I hurried along the horse trail toward Great Thumb Spring (knowing I could not reach it before dark, but confident now for the morning), my eye caught brown movement away to the right. Suddenly, close and electric, the thunder of hooves. Almost at once, the thundering died. The horse stood facing me, curious, its white blaze like a torch in the evening shadow. Then it was once more thundering up and away across the talus, back into the lingering sunset. Its hoofbeats grew fainter. Its dark shape began to merge with the shadows. And then, as it crossed the skyline, it stopped and looked back at me. To its left, the cliff was a black wall against red sky. The skirting talus swept down and away, paused, then curved upward again to an isolated hillock. The horse stood framed between cliff and hillock, etched against the sun's afterglow. I could see its pricked ears, feel their nervousness. As I stood watching, with the horse poised and tense, a hummingbird whirred brief greetings a foot from my eyes. I found myself smiling at it. When it dipped away my eyes followed its flight and I saw beyond it the white cliffs of Great Thumb Mesa. But the cliffs were no longer white. They burned now with the deep red sunset glow of the desert, the glow that catches your breath and quietens the striving and makes you want to manacle time so that the beauty can go on and on and on. For long moments I stood watching the cliffs. At last I glanced back over my shoulder. The horse had gone. And when I looked at the cliffs again the glow had already begun to die. But it did not matter now. The moment would always be there.

I walked on a little way down the trail, then camped inside the radiating warmth of a huge boulder. And soon after sunrise next morning I came to Great Thumb Spring.

The trail dipped down into a gully. All at once, thirty feet ahead, a trickle of water gleamed on red rock. And suddenly the sun was shining through a clump of scarlet Indian paintbrush and cool air was brushing over my skin and birds were murmuring in the foliage of a cottonwood tree. And at that moment I knew again—differently from the moment of the wild horse in the half-light, but with the same sure promise—that, given time, I would find in the Canyon the things I had come for.

When I reached Great Thumb Spring there were still more than three days left to the airdrop, and there was never really much doubt in my mind that I would take the drop in Fossil Bay, beyond the three critical amphitheaters. At first, faint question marks hung over feet and weather. But by the evening of the second day that I rested at the spring I could walk in something bordering on comfort (thanks largely to my having brought soft moccasins for wear around camp); and light rain showers were cooling the air and filling new rainpockets. By nine thirty on the third morning, in weather still pleasantly crisp and promisingly unsettled, I stood on the lip of the first amphitheater.

It was an impressive place. The Esplanade tapered abruptly to a narrow terrace that hung between two cliffs as if it had merely paused there, waiting for a heavy storm to send it crashing on downward. The scrub-covered talus sloped at a horrifying angle. And below its lip the rock plunged almost sheer for fifteen hundred feet. Now that I had seen the place I under-

stood why the far side of the amphitheater was big-
horn-sheep country.*

Now, it is one thing to be the first man somewhere
and quite another to know, or to be almost sure, that
you are only the second. I knew, or half-knew, that
one man had already crossed that forbidding amphitheater. Had crossed it only a week earlier. But I don't
think I realized until afterward what a difference the
knowledge made. Instead of hanging back on my men-
tal heels and wondering if the thing were really possible I just checked the route through binoculars and
then moved out onto the terrace.

For a hundred yards the talus sloped quite gently.
A faint horse trail still wound through the sparse
scrub. Then, abruptly, the talus steepened. The trail
vanished. Almost at once I found myself crossing a
bright red gully. Slowly, I eased forward across its
eroded wall, kicking shallow footholds. Fragments of
damp dirt and gravel bounced away below. They gathered noisy speed, then vanished over the lip, suddenly
and ominously silent.

At its center the gully had worn down to hard red
earth, steep as the walls of a cutting on a mountain

---

*Bighorns can cross the amphitheater, but the wild horses apparently
cannot. The bighorns seem to value privacy above almost everything, and
they choose to stay in their fastness on the far side.
    At the amphitheater, then, I had arrived at the end of the wild-horse
country. Along the Esplanade I had made seventeen horse-sightings: at least
ten different animals, including one foal. Unlike the sad beast I had photographed above Supai, all were in excellent condition. Their coloring varied from bay through chestnut to white. There was also one that looked
remarkably like a mule. They were mostly, I suppose, somewhat on the
small side, but none of them could by any stretch of the imagination be
called "miniature." Those that I saw traveled either singly or in bands of
four or five. Their immediate reaction on seeing me was to run, but after
they had put two or three hundred yards between us curiosity tempered
fear. One band even showed signs of coming back to investigate; but timidity finally triumphed.
    And that, I am afraid, is the sum total of what I learned at first hand
about the so-called miniature horses of Grand Canyon.

road. The only holds were a few half-embedded stones. I hesitated. Then, remembering Harvey Butchart, I began to ease forward again. I was agonizingly conscious now of the terrace lip, down below my feet, and of the silent space beyond it. For three or four yards each delicately balanced step was a tense and breathless movement—the kind of movement that opens up, if you are as timid a climber as I am, a trap door in the floor of your stomach. Then the red earth was past. And then the gully was past. And instead of reaching out with tense fingertips I could keep on balance merely by digging my staff into the loose talus.

I did not know at the time, of course, that the red gully was the worst of it. But nothing else quite matched those few yards across its center. All morning, though, I had to move slowly. Very slowly. Each step was the kind you took no chances with. By the time I climbed clear of the first amphitheater it was almost one o'clock.

But long before that I found myself relaxed enough to notice much more than the way ahead. To notice that horse tracks had finally given way to the scattered imprints of cloven feet. To pause after an unexpected hailstorm and find myself seeing new rainpockets on a distant rock terrace less as safety markers than as the essential elements in a cool and beautiful blue pattern. Not merely to register, when for the first time in a week I glimpsed the Colorado two thousand feet below, that some engineering manipulation at the distant upstream dam must account for the dramatic change in its color but also to feel deep pleasure at the way its sullen brown surface had been transformed into a brilliant blue. To rest beside a precariously balanced boulder and contemplate the huge, harmonic sweep of rock that plunged down to the river, paused, and then swept up again in gigantic counterstatement. To find myself, long after the halt should have ended, still sitting beside the boulder and fondling with the fingertips of my mind the texture and color and tilted pattern of cliff and hanging terrace and then cliff again. And to find that soon afterward I had stopped deep in the inner recesses of the amphitheater to admire a fragile white desert primrose that thrust up at my feet from a desolation of rubble. The need to hurry kept trying to brush aside these softer moments, but its success remained marginal.

After the red gully there were only two more really big moments that day. Neither was quite the kind I had expected.

The first lasted barely fifteen seconds.

I was walking along an easy rock terrace that led to the second amphitheater. Swirling cloud had closed down, obliterating another magnificent, plunging view of the Inner Gorge and leaving me to pick my way forward among shadowy rock shapes. It was like tramping across a Scottish moor in midwinter.

I think I saw movement first. Anyway, I know that suddenly I was peering at a vague form that stood forty or fifty yards way, on the brink of the precipice. For an instant the animal was peering back at me, tense and expectant. But almost at once it bounded away.

Then I saw something else.

It was closer than the other had been. Barely thirty yards away. Motionless on the brink of the precipice, silhouetted against swirling cloud, it seemed less an animal than a presence. A magnificent green presence. A stately, sculptured statue. For a long time we stared at each other, the statue and I, and I had time to understand that the greenness was in the massive horns that curled almost full circle. Had time to grasp that the dignity came from the horns too. From the horns and from the superb set of the head. Very slowly, I began to reach for my binoculars. Unhurriedly, the bighorn turned. After that magnificent head, its white rump looked rather ridiculous. But the beast moved with unruffled dignity, with a slow and liquid grace. It moved away from me for three or four yards. And then it was gone. Not helter-skelter gone but fading-and-merging gone, so that it was there one moment and somehow not there the next, and once more I stood alone in the swirling Scottish gloom.

The other big moment of the day had something eerie about it too.

I had crossed the second amphitheater, and then the third. Both were steep, but neither was as difficult as the first. All day, rain squalls and hailstorms had been sweeping down from the northwest. In midafternoon the air began to grow colder. And as I came out at last, about five o'clock, onto the broad rock terrace that led to Fossil Bay, snow began to fall.

Snowflakes quickly covered the sandy, chocolate-brown earth that lined the bigger rock basins. Soon the flakes were beginning to settle on the wet rock too. Once again, as had happened in the morning beyond Mount Sinyala, I found myself walking through a hushed white world of vague shapes and muffled horizons.

And then, as I padded on half an inch of snow across one of the earth-filled basins, beginning to feel a little tired at last, I stopped dead. Ahead of me across the snow, dark and definite and impossible, stretched a line of human footprints. Each print stood out sharp and clear. And the line cut straight and purposeful, like a pre-echo of my own trail, out and away into the gloom.

I stood motionless in the thickly falling snow, star-

ing, trying to reconcile what I saw with what I knew.
The footprints were undeniable. But it seemed impossible that someone was walking just ahead of me
across that remote and desolate rock terrace. Was
walking such a short way ahead that the snow had
not even begun to dull the outline of his tracks. I
peered into the whiteness, trying to push back the horizon. All day I had been savoring the knowledge that
I was the second man to pass this way. Perhaps even
the first. And now, it seemed, the place was public.

I knelt down and examined one of the footprints. It
was genuine enough. But almost at once I understood.
All around the imprint, minute pinnacles formed the
surface of the undisturbed earth. The snowflakes were
straddling the peaks of these pinnacles and building
into a thick white carpet. But within the imprint the
boot's weight had compacted the earth into a hard
and relatively smooth pan. This pan tended to hold
the recent rain, and as each snowflake landed the collected moisture dissolved it. I examined the edges of
the footprint. Wind and water had dulled their definition. Had, perhaps, been eroding the outline for a
week.

I stood up, smiling. When I walked on through the
snowstorm, following the dark imprints into the
gloom, I found that my tiredness had gone. It was
good to know, beyond any real shadow of doubt, that
I was following, with a most artistic symbolism, the
footsteps of the man who had blazed my trail and who
had, a week before, fulfilled a seventeen-year ambition. But there was more to it, I think, than feeling
glad for Harvey's sake. I found something obscurely
yet warmly companionable about these footsteps. And
their meaning was so delayed that they did not even
begin to blur the solitude.

My exhilaration outlasted the snowstorm and then

the sleet that was falling two hours later when I holed up at dusk under an overhang, within easy striking distance of Fossil Bay. It was still there next morning when I swung around into the bay in brilliant sunshine that had quickly canceled the overnight snow. And it was still there, reinforced by anticipation, when I began, about nine thirty, to prepare for the airdrop.

First I spread out my bright-orange sleeping bag, which Ranger Jim Bailey and the pilot would be looking for. Then I collected firewood and filled two of my cooking pots with water for making smoke signals to indicate which way the wind was blowing. And finally, in the suddenly tense minutes that were left, I practiced yet again the technique of sighting my extended thumb on a distant object (representing the plane) and with a small mirror aiming the sun's reflected rays partly onto the thumbtip, partly into thin air. I had never taken an airdrop before, but back in Flagstaff the pilot had shown me how to signal this way. In sunny weather, he said, he would see the flashes from miles away. It was partly his confidence in the mirror that made me decide at the last minute to take the drop two miles short of the proposed alternate site at the head of Fossil Bay, at a place that was not only more convenient for me—because I wanted to make a reconnaissance from that point, down into Fossil Canyon—but also seemed much safer for the plane's low approach run.

The zero hour I had arranged with Jim Bailey was ten o'clock. At one minute to zero I heard the sound of a motor. The little Cessna—silvery, with unmistakable red wing tips—came in higher than I had expected. I began to flash with the mirror. The plane came on. Came on. Came on. It passed directly overhead, still high, without a recognition rock of its wing tips. And then it was droning on and away and I was standing, astonished, on the red rock terrace.

The plane passed over Great Thumb Mesa and began to circle, slowly losing height. I could imagine Jim Bailey peering down at the cottonwood tree that marked Great Thumb Spring—the spring I had camped beside two nights before, the spring that was our primary dropping site. The plane vanished behind the mesa, but I could still hear it circling. And I could imagine Jim Bailey shouting at the pilot: "Looks like he hasn't made it!"

I waited, pacing up and down the red rock terrace.

Ten minutes, and they were back. They passed high above the head of Fossil Bay, then banked toward me. The plane droned overhead, ignored my frantic flashing, then began to skirt Great Thumb Point, following the rock terrace and amphitheaters that I had crossed the day before. Soon it vanished again.

For a while I could still hear its faint drone. Then the Canyon was silent with the silence I had grown used to and I knew they were searching along the Esplanade. They would probably go as far back as Supai. I no longer cared to think about what Jim Bailey was saying.

The minutes dragged by. Ten. Twenty. Thirty. The sun beat down on the red rock. I tried not to think about the sparse food reserves in my pack.

They came back at last, still high. The moment they cleared Great Thumb Mesa I lit the fire. The plane droned on, apparently heading for Grand Canyon Village and home. When the fire was burning briskly enough, I poured on the two waiting pots of water. A plume of smoke rose into the clear air. Then I was once more flashing furiously with the mirror, willing the sunlight into the pilot's eye. For long, tantalizing seconds the plane held course. Then it banked toward me. Minutes later its wings rocked the recognition signal.*

The plane made three trial runs, low enough for me to see that one door had been removed to make the drop easier. On the fourth, something tumbled out of the blank door space. A bright-orange parachute cracked open. For brief seconds it was floating, full and calm and beautiful, against blue sky. Then the cardboard-wrapped can that hung from it touched down, barely a hundred feet from my sleeping bag. The chute collapsed. I ran toward it.

The plane came back once more, still low. I butter-flied "All's well" with my arms. Wing tips rocked. Then the little Cessna was dwindling into the distance and I stood alone once more in the sunshine and the silence.

---

*At the time I wondered whether the smoke or the mirror had done the job. Much later, I asked Jim Bailey. "The smoke," he said. "I picked it up right away. And just as well. We were running for home, like you thought. We didn't see the mirror until we were almost on top of you, just before we rocked our wings. At a guess, I'd say you didn't shake the mirror enough. You've got to do that to set up a good flashing. Another trouble was that your orange sleeping bag didn't show up at all against that red rock. We could hardly see it, even on the drop run."

But at least the day taught me one valuable lesson: never change your dropping site. As for the ground signal: on the two later airdrops I had in my pack the white plastic sheet I had used on the Inner Gorge reconnaissance. I spread it out flat. Each time, the pilot saw it immediately, and there was no occasion, or even opportunity, for me to use the mirror.

TRANSITION

——

AS I stood watching the plane contract to a speck and finally dissolve in the blue distance, I think I already knew that my journey had moved on. It was no picnic yet, let alone a pilgrimage. But I had taken the critical steps. I had crossed the amphitheaters. And by taking my airdrop at the alternate site I had proved beyond all reasonable doubt that I could meet the Canyon's physical challenge.

It was not until evening, though, just after sunset, that I really grasped what the airdrop had meant. I was stretched out on top of my sleeping bag and doing nothing but gaze up into the pale sky when, far overhead, a jet airliner glinted briefly in the rays of the already hidden sun. But the plane was flying so high that its whisper did not really damage the silence. And its remote presence did not even touch the solitude.

And all at once I realized that the airdrop had not touched my solitude either. Had not penetrated my cocoon of peace and simplicity. For there had been no feeling of personal contact. Even on the Cessna's final run I had, curiously, seen no figures in the plane's cabin. And I realized now that I had not really connected the plane and its roar with actual happenings in the outside world. I had seen it as a mere convenience. As an impersonal instrument fulfilling my personal needs. And now, looking up at the remote speck that was the airliner, I saw, in the sudden and overwhelming way you do when the obvious at last forces itself on your awareness, that the important thing was my cocoon of peace and solitude. The fact that a cocoon existed. I had, I saw, finally escaped from the paradox of simple living. The trivia were still there, and would be until the end of my journey. But I had overcome them. Had broken free at last from the din and deadline of the outside world.

I promptly held a celebration: I prefaced dinner with the week's menu-spicing delicacy, a can of smoked sliced lobster, and afterward I tempered the pemmican and dehydrated potatoes with claret. At the meal's end, for a semidelightful five minutes, I was half-canyons over.*

Yet the turning point that I had sensed did not immediately materialize. I even managed to spend the next three days pressed tighter than ever to the sweaty world of effort.

All through those three days I reconnoitered, hard, in Fossil Canyon. No one, it seemed, had ever found a way down this narrow cleavage in the rock, almost two thousand feet deep. But I knew that if I succeeded I would be able to travel beside the Colorado and avoid the appallingly long and apparently waterless extension of the Esplanade that still separated me from the cache

---

*Only semidelightful. Although the delicacies were a pleasing change at every cache and drop, the claret never quite seemed to add the final touch I had hoped for. I have since realized that you don't really need alcohol in the wilderness. Not when you're alone, anyway.

I had hidden just below the Rim near Bass Camp. (As far as I knew this terrace was quite without any natural water source; but halfway along, just below the Rim at Apache Point, I had put out my only other cache, and it included four gallons of water.)

The idea of pioneering a route down Fossil Canyon had attracted me at least as much as the practical advantages, and for three days, based on my airdrop camp, I walked and scrambled and climbed and inched my way down and along and then back and along and then across and up and along an endless succession of terraces and ledges and cliffs. Twice I followed tapering cliff-face cracks until I was out in places I should never have been. And there was one talus slope I hope some day to forget. On the third evening I came back to camp exhausted. My left hand was a throbbing pin cushion: in a sudden moment of fear, on a sloping rockledge strewn with rubble, I had grabbed blindly for a handhold and found a prickly pear. And for the third straight day I had failed to find a break in the Redwall cliff that is Fossil Canyon's major barrier.

It was as I lay in my mummy bag waiting for dinner to cook that I realized that by concentrating on the reconnaissance I had lost sight of why I had come down into the Canyon. Once the idea had occurred to me, the stupidity of the mistake became quite clear. And I decided immediately that I would rest for two days beside the large rainpocket at the head of Fossil Bay—the rainpocket that had been the proper alternate drop site—and then strike out along the terrace toward Bass Camp.

That decision was the real turning point.

I do not mean that I discovered at once the things I had come to find. But from then on I moved steadily toward them. Moved closer to rock and sky, to light and shadow, to space and silence. Began to feel their rhythms.

Of course, the change did not appear clear-cut. If you had asked me at almost any time during that week how the journey was progressing I would have answered, I think, with reports on water supply and condition of feet and quantity of food left and distance remaining to the next cache. These were still the things I measured progress by. Most of the time, anyway.

On this important and insistent level, the week was a period of steady and straightforward physical progress. I rested as planned for almost two full days beside the deep rainpocket at the head of Fossil Bay, then struck south. The terrace that led to Bass Camp was four times as long as the one I had barely managed to complete on that first Butchart test day to Sinyala Canyon, and even with my halfway cache at Apache Point it looked as if it would be the toughest leg so far. But now I was ten days better tuned, and the operation went off exactly according to plan.

I left the head of Fossil Bay in the cool of evening, as I usually do when a long day lies ahead. I carried three gallons of water and camped barely two hours out. By six o'clock next evening I had crossed the precipitous head of Forster Canyon—a barrier that wild burros cannot pass, and which marks the eastern limit of the bighorn country, just as the amphitheater under Great Thumb Mesa marks its western limit. At nightfall I camped close under Apache Point, on the first map-marked trail since Supai. This Apache Trail, though betraying no hint of human use, turned out to be a busy burro turnpike (the burros are the National Park's unpaid trail maintenance crew) and I made good time along it. By noon next day I had reached and found unharmed the five-gallon can of supplies and the four gallons of bottled water that formed my cache at Apache Point. (I arrived with only 65 cc. of water left, but the situation was much less critical than it sounds: before climbing the steep thousand-foot talus slope below the cache I had lightened my load by drinking most of the quite adequate supply left in my canteens.) In the cool of that evening I carried three gallons of water back down to the terrace and camped. Next day I broke the back of the long, zigzag, burro-trail swing around Aztec Amphitheater. And by ten o'clock on the fourth morning after leaving Fossil Bay I was standing on Bass Trail with half a gallon of water left in my canteens and luxuriating in the comfortable knowledge that the Bass Camp cache lay only a thousand vertical feet above. The week's physical progress was as simple and straightforward as that.

The deeper progress of these days was even more satisfying—but neither so simple nor so straightforward. It came erratically and hesitantly, so that later I remembered the week less as a steady stream of events than as a montage of moments.

They often came, these moments, quite unexpectedly.

About ten o'clock on the morning after I had abandoned the Fossil Canyon reconnaissance I was breaking my airdrop camp in leisurely fashion for the move to the head of Fossil Bay when I noticed a small green-speckled lizard move speculatively out from a crack in the red rock. Jerkily, with many interrogatory genuflections, it investigated my toothbrush. Then it strolled across my outspread washcloth, mounted the stone that was holding it down, closed its eyes, and basked. I went quietly about my business. Quarter of an hour, and the lizard opened its eyes. A minute passed before it moved; but when it did it no longer strolled. It flicked forward; halted; inspected the world; riveted its attention on a shrub; rocketed toward it; leaped. The leap carried it a full five inches off the ground. At least, I received the impression of a five-inch jump. But all I really saw was a blur—and then a re-landed lizard smacking its lips and looking very pleased with itself and obviously more than ready for another fly if one should be so ill-advised as to settle within jumping range.

Now, every sunlit desert morning has a magic moment. It may come at five o'clock, at seven, or at eleven, depending on the weather and the season. But it comes. If you are in the right mood at the right time you are suddenly aware that the desert's countless cogs have meshed. That the world has crystallized into vivid focus. And you respond. You hold your breath or fall into a reverie or spring to your feet, according to the day and the mood.

The leaping lizard heralded such a moment. I do not mean that anything very dramatic happened. A waspish-banded fly took a hovering look at my nylon rope, then snapped away into invisibility. A butterfly landed on one of my red socks. A hummingbird buzzed the sock and the butterfly flickered, vanished. The hummingbird cased the orange parachute, rejected it, up-tailed away to a nearby bush, and perched there with constant nervous quiverings of its violet-banded neck. That was all, I suppose. That, and a sharpening of the sunlight, a thickening of wind-borne scents, or perhaps a deeper vibration somewhere down in the silence. But I know that all at once, standing there on the red rock terrace, still watching the lizard, I was knife-edge alive.

It did not last, of course. They cannot last, these climax moments. In five minutes or ten or thirty the heat begins. Gently at first, then harshly, it clamps down on the desert, stifling the day's vitality. And you sink back from your peak of awareness. In a little while, that sunlit morning on the red rock terrace, I sank slowly and sadly back; but afterward, all through the two days I rested beside the big rainpocket at the head of Fossil Bay, I remained aware of simple things that the trivia had been smothering. I stood in silence beneath the curving harmony of three huge sandstone boulders. I wondered what lived down a tiny vertical shaft in hot red sand. I even found myself listening to birdsong, which is not, I'm afraid to say, my habit. Found myself really listening—to a piercing intermittent blast so like a referee's whistle that it kept stopping me in my tracks; and to a soft, contemplative warble that repeated, endlessly: "Years and years and years and years and years . . ."

When I saw another bighorn sheep—clear and sharp this time, in sunlight, and quite close—I realized that I had come to understand something about the lives of these graceful and dignified creatures. I am not talking now about hard zoological facts. Not even about such practical information as that these nimble-footed individualists are mediocre trailmakers. (Their most heavily used highway never amounted to much more than a suggestion that a couple of little bighorns might have passed that way in Indian file about the time of Custer's last stand.) I am thinking of less tangible matters.

During my reconnaissance of Fossil Canyon, cloven tracks in rain-smoothed sand pockets had shown me that bighorns travel by preference along the brinks of precipices. I had discovered too that they choose their hideouts, or at least their habitual lying-down places, far out along perilously inaccessible rockledges. Most of the heavily patrolled precipices and all the hideouts commanded magnificent, sweeping panoramas of the kind that no man can look at unmoved. After a day or two it occurred to me that the bighorns' choice might be no coincidence; and the more I thought about it, the more difficult I found it to avoid the idea that these dignified animals appreciate scenic beauty.*

During the two day's rest at the head of Fossil Bay I even found myself looking differently at inanimate objects. Brooding over the map, I found that instead of worrying only about the way ahead I was reading history. The map—a work of art as well as an astonishingly accurate cartographic document—eased me, step by step, into the past.

The survey which produced the map was begun in 1902 by one François Matthes and was finally completed in 1923. I could grasp this date fairly firmly: I was born in 1922. Stanton Point carried me back around the turn of the century: in 1889 and 1890, Robert Brewster Stanton was first a member and then the leader of two survey parties that investigated a part

---

*For many decades now zoologists have been reacting in justifiable concert against those purple outpourings of the last century which tended to equate simple animal behavior with complicated human activity. But perhaps they have leaned backward too far. The incessant and almost automatic accusations of "Anthropomorphism!" are beginning to sound familiar. In other places they shout "Communism!" or "Capitalism!"

There are signs, fortunately, of a corrective swing; but most present-day zoologists would still sniff at my "insight" into bighorn psychology. "Protection from predators," they would intone, "demands inaccessible resting places and maximal visibility." Plausible, of course, but not altogether convincing. What real practical advantage stems from being able to look out over a distant landscape in which any enemy you see is already held at bay by an impassable cliff? And why should aesthetics not have evolved in mammals quite independently of daub-minded monkeys or their more self-conscious successors? We are all made, broadly speaking, of the same flesh and blood and nerve ends.

At the very least, it is pleasing to feel that the zoologists may in the end turn out to be wrong.

(Some time after I had written this footnote I was delighted to find solid support for my suggestion in Sally Carrighar's provocative book *Wild Heritage*. And the trend away from the shibboleth of "Anthropomorphism!" continues. Recently we have had the even more fundamentally challenging *On Aggression* by Konrad Lorenz, a zoologist with a worldwide reputation. Also the more popularly written *Territorial Imperative* by Robert Ardrey. Naturally, both books have been savagely attacked.)

of the Colorado on behalf of an optimistic railroad company, and lost three men by drowning within six days; not altogether surprisingly, he failed to convince anyone that they should build a railroad through the Canyon. I map-dreamed on, and Bass Trail and Hance Trail took me back another decade: in the late 1880's and early 1890's two miners named William Bass and John Hance, quite independently and in different parts of the Canyon, began to turn from mining to dude wrangling and so begat the local tourist industry. Other place names recalled key figures in the Canyon's white-man history: Powell Plateau honors the one-armed Major John Wesley Powell who in 1869 led the river party that forced the first passage of the Canyon and who later became director of the United States Geological Survey; and Ives Point commemorates the efforts of Lieutenant Joseph Christmas Ives, who in 1857 led the first government exploration of the area.* And Cardenas Butte was obviously named for García López de Cárdenas, one of Coronado's captains, who led the party that "discovered" the Canyon in October 1540.

Other names on the map probed back more deeply, though less obviously, into time. A man who gave buttes and pinnacles such names as Vishnu Temple and Krishna Shrine and Tower of Ra and Wotan's Throne had clearly been moved to feelings beyond the here and now. But religion is not the only mystery that can move a man. Near the head of Bass Trail lay Darwin Plateau. From its northern rim ran Huxley and Spencer Ter-

---

*In his report to Congress, Ives perpetrated a masterpiece of malprognostication: "Ours has been the first and will doubtless be the last party of whites to visit this profitless locality. It seems intended by nature that the Colorado River, along the greater portion of its lonely and majestic way, shall be forever unvisited and undisturbed."
Today, over a million people a year visit the Rims of Grand Canyon. And the Colorado is, unfortunately, anything but undisturbed.

races. And between them, sure enough, nestled Evolution Amphitheater. As I brooded over the map, there beside the rainpocket at the head of Fossil Bay, it seemed to me that these last names were the ones that carried the heaviest load of meaning.

Sometimes now I found myself thinking, quite specifically, about the longer time spans.

From the earliest planning days I had expected that as I walked I would ponder a great deal about the rock. After all, the Canyon is above everything else a geological phenomenon. But it had not happened this way. The rock had always been there, but by and large my eye had seen only its surface. Had seen only route and obstacle, shape and shadow, or at the most, magnificent sculpture. Back on the Esplanade, even a striking example of a toadstool rock had seemed little more than an oddity, a chance photogenic freak. I had seen, in other words, only static things, not imprints of a flowing process.

For stimulation along the way I had put in my pack a small paperback book on geology, but in the first two weeks there had been no time to do more than glance at it. But now, resting beside the big rainpocket at the head of Fossil Bay, I began to read.

Perhaps the book was one reason why, as I bathed one morning in water from the rainpocket, standing in warm and soothing sunshine, I noticed that I had a shell-patterned bathroom wall. The big white boulder had broken away quite recently, I saw, from the cliffs above. Less than a million years ago, certainly. Probably no more than a few hundred thousand years ago. Perhaps it had even fallen since that yesterday in which García López de Cárdenas and his party stood awestruck on the Rim. And as I stood wet and naked in the sunshine, looking down at the shells that were

now fossils (they looked exactly like our modern cockleshells), I found myself understanding, vividly and
effortlessly, that they had once been the homes of sen-
tient, breathing creatures that had lived out their lives
on a dark and ancient ocean floor and in the end had
died there. Slowly, year after year, their empty shells
had been buried by the minute specks that are always
settling to the floor of any ocean (specks that are
themselves often the shells of tiny creatures that have
also lived and felt and died). For a moment I could
visualize this drama quite clearly, even though what
had once been the slowly building ocean floor was now
four hundred feet of solid limestone high above my
head, gleaming white in the desert sunlight. I could
feel the actuality so clearly that the wetness of that
ancient ocean was almost as real to me as the wetness
of the water on my body. I could not comprehend in
any meaningful way *when* all this had happened, for
I knew that those shells in my bathroom wall had lived
and died 200 million years before I came to wash beside them; and 200 million years, I had to admit, still
lay beyond my grasp. But after the moment of understanding had passed, as it soon did, I knew with certainty that in its own good time the Canyon would
show me the kind of geology I had hoped to find.

The evening I struck south from Fossil Bay, the look
and challenge of the terrace that stretched out ahead,
on and on, inevitably screwed my mind back to the
present. Two hours out, as night fell, I camped—
because it happened at that moment to become too
dark to go on—beside a dead juniper tree. "Damn!" my
notebook complained. "Back to press, press, press.
Back to Butcharting." But by nine o'clock next morning I had covered half the straight-line distance between Fossil and Apache, and the pressure began to

ease. Then, as I swung around an outcrop and for the first time that morning came to the very lip of the terrace, I stopped in my tracks.

Since leaving Supai I had glimpsed the Colorado only briefly, a short segment at a time, framed deep in the V of a sidecanyon. It had remained remote, cut off from my terrace world. But now there opened up at my feet a huge and unexpected space. On the floor of this space, three thousand feet below, flowed the river. It flowed directly toward me, uninterrupted, down the long and arrowlike corridor of a tremendous gorge.

The whole colossal scene was filled and studded and almost ignited by the witchery of desert sunlight, and the Gorge no longer looked at all a terrible place. Compared with the gloomy chasm in which I had made my reconnaissance, it seemed broad and open and inviting. Now the Colorado no longer swirled brown and sullen; its bright blue surface shone and sparkled. And although the river lay far below me I found that it no longer existed in a totally different world.

Yet because of the size and the beauty and the brilliance of this magnificently unexpected view I felt in that first moment on the lip of the terrace something of the shock that had overwhelmed me when I first stood, a year earlier, on the Rim of the Canyon. It even seemed that, once again, I was meeting the silence—the silence I thought I had grown accustomed to—as something solid, face to face. And just for a moment I felt once more the same understanding and acceptance of the vast, inevitable sweep of geologic time.

The understanding did not last, of course. I was too firmly embedded that morning in the hours and the minutes (though I stayed for almost an hour, gazing at and then photographing that stupendous corridor, which the map calls Conquistador Aisle). But when I walked on eastward again—hurrying a little now, to make up for lost time—I remembered that moment of shock when I first saw the corridor open up in front of me. And I knew that, like the shell pattern in my bathroom wall, the moment had been a promise.

There is something of a gap, then, in my montage of moments. For the next two days, in unbroken sunshine and growing heat, it was all yard and mile, minute and hour; zig and then zag and then zig again along terrace and talus, terrace and talus, terrace and talus; a scrambling, sweaty climb to Apache Point; the long swing around Aztec Amphitheater. But the cool of each evening was an intermission.

The first of these nights I camped—again because that was where I happened to run out of daylight—beside a big juniper tree. As I went to sleep, black branches curved up and over against the stars. The next night I once more camped beside a juniper tree. This time, I camped there because it grew on the brink of a precipice that promised magnificent moonlight vistas. I lit no fire, so that nothing would block me off from the night. And before I went to sleep I sat and watched the promised vistas materialize, gloriously, and felt the hours of sweat and effort sink back and away.

The third night I stumbled on one of those strokes of luck that you seem almost able to count on when things are going well.

I had not actually run short of water; but by dusk I was conscious that I would have to drink a little sparingly until I reached my Bass Camp cache, sometime next day. Then, as the burro trail I was following skirted a smooth shelf of rock, I saw out of the corner of my eye what seemed in the failing light to be the glint of dampness. I stopped, took two paces backward. Above the dampness, half-concealed, a tiny pool of water. Nothing more. I drew a finger across the dampness. For a moment there was a causeway of dry rock. Then moisture had welled over again, slowly but without hesitation, and erased it.

I held my breath and listened. A rhythmic rippling of the silence, barely perceptible. I climbed down a few feet of layered rock below the dampness and found, sure enough, a little overhang; and when I put a cooking pot beneath it the metallic and monotonous drip, drip, drip of the single drops of water made beautiful and moving music.

I camped ten feet from the seep, beside a white-flowering bush that overhung a precipice. From my bedside the bush framed with Japanese delicacy an immense blue-black pit that was filled not so much with shapes as with suggestions of shapes—gargantuan shapes that would have been deeply disturbing if I had not known by heart now exactly what they meant.

That night, again, I lit no fire. And as I sat waiting for dinner to cook—cut off from the silence, inside the roaring world of my little stove—I watched the evening sky grow dark. Slowly the darkness deepened. But the blue-black pit below me remained blue-black. Began, even, to ease back from the brink of blackness. For as the last daylight sank away, the moon took over, casting shadows at new angles, constructing new shapes, warding off the blackness with a new and cool and exquisitely delicate blue.

When I took dinner off the stove I found myself looking at the fire ring, shining red-hot out of the darkness. Found myself, unexpectedly, appreciating that it too was a thing of beauty and value. And when I turned off the stove I heard all around me, as always happens, the sudden and surprising silence.

While I ate dinner, with the silent blue-black pit opening up below me, I found myself savoring the sense of newness and expectancy that now came with every step of my journey—the always-moving-forward that now filled each day of my life. Soon, I began to contemplate the clock that measured this daily progress; and all at once I was feeling, as if I had never understood it before, the swing and circle of the sun. Sunrise and sunset; sunrise and sunset; sunrise again; and then sunset. It happened everywhere, of course, all over the earth. But now I could detect in the beat of that rhythm an element I had never felt before. Now I could feel the inevitability of it. An inevitability that was impersonal and terrifying and yet, in the end, comforting. And as I sat looking out over the huge and mysterious blue-black space it occurred to me that the pioneers who crossed the American prairies in their covered wagons must have felt, many days out from sight of mountains, the power of this ceaseless rhythm. For them the understanding would have been generated by the monotony of the plains. For me it had something to do with the colossal sameness of the Canyon; but that was a sameness not of monotony but of endlessly repeated yet endlessly varied pattern. A prodigal repetition of terrace mounting on terrace mounting on terrace, of canyon after canyon after canyon after canyon. All of them, one succeeding the other, almost unknown to man, just existing, existing, existing, existing. There seemed at first no hope of a beginning, no hint of an end. But I knew now, more certainly and more easily, that the regularity and the existence were not really timeless. I knew they were echoing reminders of a time, not so very long ago, before the coming of the noisy animal, when the earth was a quiet place.

When I had finished my dinner I lay still and listened to the silence. To the silence and to the music of the water splashing metronomically down into my cooking pot. Before I fell asleep—warm and comfortable inside my mummy bag, passively at ease now inside the silence and the darkness—I knew that at last I stood on the threshold of the huge natural museum that is Grand Canyon.

You cannot, of course, enter such a museum without preparation. It is not a mere place of knowledge. It is not really a place at all, only a state of understanding. As I lay in the darkness, staring up at the stars and hearing how the silence was magnified by the drip, drip, drip of water, I knew that after all my days of effort and silence and solitude I was almost ready at last to move inside the museum.

But a journey is always, before anything else, a physical thing.

By ten o'clock next morning I had begun to climb up Bass Trail toward my cache. In his note with the airdrop Ranger Jim Bailey had said that he might be near Bass Camp on park business somewhere about this date and might be able to check whether I had found the cache. But I knew that he would hardly come down into the Canyon to look for me: it would be like combing Africa for Livingstone, and no natives to question. I climbed up the steep trail, watching the red terrace unfold below, watching it grow less red with distance and more and more orange. I turned onto the last twisting stretch of trail before my cache. And then, all at once, there was an animal, coming down toward me. A broad, green animal. A large animal, walking upright.

My voice sounded strange. It was the first time I had heard it in two weeks.

"Mr. Stanley, I presume," it said.

"Well I'll be damned!" said Jim Bailey.

ROCK

WE SAT and talked—Jim Bailey and a Park naturalist and I—beside the shallow limestone cave in which
I had hidden my cache, and for an hour the world
beyond the Rim was almost for real. For behind everything they said I heard murmurs of a life hemmed
in by authority and convention, by money-thrust, by
conflicting loyalties, by today and tomorrow.

But when they went back up over the Rim they took
the murmurs with them. And soon it was as if they
had never sat with me beside the cave, and I moved
back into my own world. I watched a tiny red spider
scurry mad patterns on a stone. I ran my hand over
the layered white walls of the limestone cave. I let
myself ride with the cloud shadows, far below, across
Darwin Plateau and up the white dome called Mount
Huethawali and out over the dark Inner Gorge and
then on and over the sun-baked rock terraces until at
last we soared up and out and away beyond the distant white cliffs that were the North Rim.

In late afternoon I transferred into my canteens,
very carefully, the water from the two-gallon-size wine
bottles that formed part of the cache; and, because I

had immediate plans for the five-gallon can that held the next week's supplies, I stuffed it, still unpacked, into my pack bag. In the cool of evening I started back down Bass Trail.

There was no hurry now. I had food for a week, and the Trail led directly down to the river and the safety of unlimited water. I walked slowly, stopping when I wanted to. I stopped to look, unsuccessfully, for some ancient cliff dwellings the naturalist had mentioned. I stopped to look, also unsuccessfully, for cockleshells and other fossils in the white beds of limestone. And when I moved down out of limestone into sandstone—the same pale brown sandstone that had quietened me on the first evening of my journey, below Hualpai Hilltop—I stopped for a moment to consider with some surprise that ever since I climbed up onto the terrace above Supai, two weeks earlier, I had followed the same red layers of interleaved shale and sandstone that I had climbed up onto above Supai. On the two brief occasions I had left these layers—the reconnaissance of Fossil Canyon and the scramble up to Apache Point—there had been no time to stand and stare. But now it would be different. I had time to walk slowly, antennae spread, down through every layer of the Canyon's sculpture, from Rim to river.

A year before, at the Visitor Center, I had learned that each of these layers was a page in the earth's autobiography. And I had learned, intellectually, that the pages, taken together, revealed more of the earth's past than you can see from any other single place on its surface. I had, of course, moved down through these same layers on my way to the Inner Gorge reconnaissance. But at that time I had not been ready to read them: I was still jangling with the stubbly rhythms of the world beyond the Rim.

I walked on down Bass Trail. It hairpinned through
the brown sandstone, just as the trail had done below
Hualpai Hilltop. And all at once I found myself standing in front of a little grotto. It was no more, really,
than a hollow eroded back into the rock; a roofed-over
shelf, ten feet long, four feet deep, and perhaps two
feet high. But in the very center of its entrance, seem-
ing to support the roof, stood a buttress. The buttress
was, I knew, merely the chance result of erosion, a
relic of rock that would in the slow and inexorable
course of time dwindle beneath the wind and water
that had carved it until at last it crumbled and vanished. But now, at this particular point in time, it was
a beautiful thing.

The buttress merged with roof and floor in flowing
and perfectly proportioned curves. And on its face was
superimposed a small, delicately sculptured column,
so oddly weathered that it seemed almost a decorative afterthought. The surface of this column was
rounded and smooth, as if it had been sandpapered
by a patient carpenter, and its fine-drawn strata stood
out sharp and clear, like the grain on unstained, highly
polished wood. The column's irregular outline flowed
quite independently of the buttress's: it meandered
upward, narrowed to a neck, then merged into a massive, curving superstructure of heavily bedded rock-
bands. And these bands, slanting down at a slight
angle to the strata of both column and buttress, dominated the grotto and fused each element of it into a
single harmony of curve and crosscut, grain and color,
light and enigmatic shade.

For a long time I stood and looked at the grotto,
feeling for something I knew was there but could not
quite reach. At last I turned and walked on down the
trail. But now, as I walked, I found myself looking
at the rock more closely, thinking it more closely,

feeling it more closely. It seemed as if all at once I could recognize, in some new and more thorough way—without any sense of revelation, just with an easy acceptance—how time, sandpapering rock, had created harmony and beauty. (But, after all, what was beauty but some kind of harmony between the rock and my senses?) And as I walked on down the trail I found that now at last I could comprehend the reality of what had happened to build the sandstone from which time had carved the grotto. I could comprehend it more than intellectually now, so that I could almost feel the dust stinging my bare legs. For the sandstone had been built by the same kind of wind and the same kind of dust that had blown at Hualpai Hilltop. The wind had whipped the dust along and then had dropped it, grain after grain, layer after layer, foot after foot—and had gone on doing so day after year after decade after century after millennium for perhaps ten million years, until at last it had built a layer of sand more than three hundred feet thick. Then the slow cementing action of water and colossal pressure had converted sand into rock. Into rock that preserved the outlines of rolling dunes as tilted strata. As strata that might stand out, where chance and time created a cliff face, as the crosscut grain on a decorative column or the slanting line of a massive rockband. A band that might, given the right random erosion, help fuse the harmonies of an exquisite little grotto. It was very simple, really. The only thing the wind and the dust needed was time.

And now I found that I was ready to grant them the time. For at last I could look, steadily, beyond today and tomorrow. And beyond yesterday. I could accept the day after century after millennium after millennium after slow millennium during which the wind had blown the dust in pale clouds across rolling sand dunes. I knew now how it had been. The dust had filled up a hollow here and a hollow there, built new dunes behind them, filled the new hollows—on and on and on, layer upon layer, until the sand lay three hundred feet thick. Then some slow, chance movement of the earth's crust happened to submerge the dunes beneath a shallow sea and tiny white-shelled creatures began their task of living and dying, living and dying, living and dying, until they had built above the sand the four-hundred-foot layer of limestone that now formed the Canyon's Rim. Yes, it was very simple, really. And now I could accept it all, without effort and as a part of my natural range of thought. As a part of my natural range of thought, that was the important thing.

I came down out of the sandstone onto familiar red rock and walked across Darwin Plateau. And as the light failed I camped close under the white dome of Mount Huethawali, quite near Huxley Terrace and only just around the corner from Evolution Amphitheater.

I camped, for nostalgia's sake, beside a big juniper tree. The juniper grew on the brink of the Redwall, and beyond it there opened up, as there had opened up on other evenings, a gray, shape-filled pit. But this time, because I knew that in the morning I would go down into the pit, its shapes held new meaning. As darkness fell they seemed to challenge me; even, at first, to menace.

But in the morning it was different. There was an interval of superb synchronization when, at exactly the moment the moon sank behind the Rim and the pit's blue-black shadows eased over into black, a paleness began to invade the eastern sky. The shadows faded. Vague shapes crystallized, as they always did, into butte and cliff and mesa. Soon daylight had filled the pit with its colossal, solid sculpture. But when, after breakfast, I walked on down Bass Trail—acutely aware once more of the pages of the earth's autobiography—I no longer looked at the sculpture. Instead, my eyes sought out the strata that gave the sculpture meaning.

Below my nightcamp the trail swung around to the right and angled down across the face of the Redwall in a manmade cutting. Here the story of the earth was no longer written in grains of sand. The smooth red rock under my feet had been built—much as the white upper limestone had been built—by the shells of minute organisms that had lived and died by the millions upon billions in an ancient sea and had gone on living and dying and sinking to the sea bed until their corpses had built a layer of blue-gray rock six hundred feet deep. A rock whose surface has been stained red by water seeping down from the red, iron-bearing strata above. Yes, it was all very simple still, and very easy to accept.

I moved down deeper into the Canyon.

Soon I was walking over interleaved layers, purple and green, of shale that had once been mud swirling down an ancient river that flowed long before the Colorado existed. Mud that had come to rest at last, thick and soft, off some primordial shore. Had come to rest in the same way that thick, soft mud is coming to rest today off the mouth of the Colorado and forming mud flats that will probably, in due time, become new layers of shale or slate.

I moved down yet deeper.

On the brink of the Inner Gorge I passed through a band of dark brown sandstone. (This time, it was sand from a beach.) And then, below the sandstone, I stepped down into a different world.

All at once, black and twisted rocks pressed in on me—rocks that had been so altered by time and heat and pressure that no one can tell for sure what their original form was. And as I walked down between them, sinking deeper into a narrow cleft that forms one of the rare major breaks in the wall of the Inner Gorge, I felt again, as I had not felt since my reconnaissance, the oppression of insignificance.

I walked on down. The cleft deepened. The black rock pressed closer, almost shutting out the sky. And then, quite suddenly, I had stepped out onto a broad rock platform. A hundred feet below me the river was sparkling blue-green and white. And the sky had opened up again.

I sat and rested on the rock platform, looking over and beyond the river at the strata on strata that mounted one on the other to the North Rim. I could see them all, every layer. They were replicas of those I had just moved down through. And after I had sat and looked at them for a while I saw that now, from a distance, I could see with eye and intellect what I had all day been understanding through instinct. Now, as my eye traveled downward from the Rim, it watched the rocks grow older.

It watched them grow older in a way that would have been impossible when I was living, day after day, surrounded and cushioned and segregated by the accouterments of the man-ruled world—by chairs and electricity and money-thrust and the rest of the tinsel. I knew that when I returned to that world I would probably remember what I saw as a flight of fancy, as airy symbolism. But at the time, as I sat there on the rock platform above the sparkling river, the pageant I saw spread out before me shone with a reality as rich as any I have ever caught in the beam of logic.

I saw, when I looked up at the Rim, that the uppermost layers of rock were bright and bold and youthful. Their unseamed faces shone pink or white or suntan-brown, untouched by the upheavals that time brings to all of us. But below the Redwall they began to show their age. There, in staid maturity, they wore dark greens and subdued browns. And their faces had begun to wrinkle. Then, as my eye reached the lip of the Inner Gorge, the rocks plunged into old age. Now they wore gray and sober black. The wrinkles had deepened. And their features had twisted beneath the terrible weight of the years. Old age had come to them, just as it comes in the end to all of us who live long enough.

I rested on the rock platform for an hour. Then I clambered down to the river through the darkest and most twisted rock of all. Once more, as on the Inner Gorge reconnaissance, every boulder and hanging fragment of the rock around me looked ready to come crashing down at any minute. But now I needed no tight and determined thinking to ward off fear. During my three weeks among crumbling rockfaces and loose talus, all apparently waiting to crash headlong at any minute, I had heard just once—a long way off— the sound of a small stone falling a very short distance. And now I understood why.

The poised boulders and fragments were indeed waiting to crash down at any minute. But there was not really too much danger that one would hit me during that particular hiccup of time we humans called May 1963. For our human clocks and the geologic clock kept different times. "Any minute now," geologic time, meant only that several fragments of rock might fall before May 2063, and that quite an appreciable number would probably do so by May 11963. I knew this now, through and through. I might not yet understand the explicit, absolute meaning of two hundred million years. But I had come to grips with the kind of geology I had hoped to find. I had begun at last to hear the rhythm of the rock.

RHYTHM

WHEN I looked back afterward at the week between Bass Trail and Phantom Ranch I could see that it had moved forward, even more clearly than life usually does, on many levels.

The physical progress was once more straightforward: two days' rest at the foot of Bass Trail, a day's reconnaissance along the Inner Gorge, then four days of steady eastward walking along the Tonto Platform—a well-defined terrace, a thousand feet above the river, that borders the Gorge east of Bass Trail.

But this surface life was by no means always the most real.

When you ferret out something for yourself, piecing the clues together unaided, it remains for the rest of your life in some way truer than facts you are merely taught, and freer from onslaughts of doubt. The multiple parallels that permeate everything we know are something I ferreted out for myself long before anyone taught me such words as microcosm and macrocosm; and beyond Bass Trail I began to find that I was not only hearing the rhythm of the rock more clearly and more certainly but was also beginning to detect point and counterpoint.

Naturally, this modulation did not take place as a sudden switch.

The week began as a diffused and untidy hodge-podge. At first I registered only a jumble of impressions, without bonds that could lock them into a coherent pattern. Then, as so often happens in the life of a journey or an isolated community, events took an unexpected turn. The unexpected events were very simple, both of them; but they seemed to act as catalysts. And a chemistry occurred. The space and the silence and the solitude and the beauty had all along been working together; now, by catalysis, they fused. I found myself living as if I were deeply immersed not merely in the physical and present Canyon but in all the slow processes that had gone into its making and had, long before that, gone into the making of its materials. It was as if I had passed into a new and echoing gallery of the natural museum that is Grand Canyon. And by the time I reached Phantom Ranch the meanings of the week had fully crystallized.

As all natural processes must, my journey had adjusted to a new state of affairs and had moved on.

For two days and three nights I camped at the foot of Bass Trail, in a little rock-bound bay beside the river.

At first, luxuriously aware that for the moment I had escaped the pressures of time and of uncertain water supply, I lay fallow. The sand of the little bay was soft and smooth, and it was good to do nothing but sprawl out on it, or on my blue but no longer pristine groundsheet. Although heavy clouds covered the sun all through the first afternoon, the temperature still climbed to over 80 degrees, and after all the long, dry days since Supai the river looked irresistibly inviting. Every hour or two I took a leisurely bath. The second day, the sun shone. But the bay never became an oven. Morning and evening, the steep rock that walled it in cast cool shadows, and in the afternoon a wind blew.

From time to time I did a few chores—the kind of chores that always seem to need doing when you at last take a rest day. I unpacked the new week's supplies from the five-gallon can that I had carried down from Bass Camp cache and assigned each item to one or other of the two pillow-size plastic food bags (one for the current day's rations, one for the balance) or to the "nibble pocket" of the pack, where I kept quick-energy snacks immediately available for use at halts. (I noted with some amusement that once again, as had happened at Supai and at the Apache Point cache, I found the new supplies strangely exciting. I am inclined to think it was mostly the look of the clean new plastic freezer bags I had packed them in.) I carefully refilled the salt-and-pepper container, the polyethylene sugar box, and the dried-milk squirter (one of those plastic, nozzle-capped containers you can buy honey or mustard or tomato catsup in). I rubbed a whole canful of wax from the cache into the scuffed and rather dried-out uppers of my boots. I gave the cooking pots a thorough scouring. I washed all clothes. I sewed a button back on the built-in adjustable belt on my corduroy shorts, using a needle with thread wound around it that traveled in my waterproof matchsafe. I also re-stitched a pack strap that was threatening to pull apart.

After some careful calculations I decided that I had

just enough food to last me for eight days rather than
a week, and so could spend an extra day getting to
Phantom Ranch. It wouldn't really be a matter of
stretching out the week's basic rations. I had arrived
at the cache with a little food still in my pack, including an eight-ounce rum fudge bar emergency ration,
now replaced by another from the cache. The cache
had also included the usual menu-varying delicacy (a
can of smoked oysters) in addition to the bottle of
claret. And then there were fish.

I was carrying a featherweight emergency fishing
kit: a spool of six-pound nylon, several BB shot, a
hook, and a 35-mm. film can of salmon eggs. Attached
to my walking staff in that order, the tackle soon extracted from one corner of my little bay about a dozen
small catfish and, after some pretty fancy staffman-
ship, a one-and-a-half-pound carp. The carp in particular, grilled on bare embers in the "aluminum foil"
jacket of its own thick scales, provided not only valuable extra calories but also a welcome change from
pemmican.*

The fire on which I cooked the fish was a small,
mealtime-only affair. It was many nights now since I
had needed a fire for warmth, or for cheer, so I rarely
built one. This was not pure laziness. A campfire, for
all its pulsating, dream-inducing fascination, cuts you
off from the reality of the night, and as the days
passed I found myself becoming less and less tolerant
of any barrier that came between me and the reality
of the Canyon.

For much of the two days I spent in my little bay,
I just sprawled on the sand and let the thoughts come

---

*Carp are newcomers to the Canyon. An Asiatic species, apparently in-
troduced at Yuma, Arizona, in the 1890's, they quickly adjusted to the new
conditions and have now spread throughout the lower and middle reaches
of the Colorado.

and go. It so happened that before I came down into the Canyon I had read, almost by accident, a little about the recent past of this particular corner of it, and my mind soon switched back from the solemn rhythms of geologic time to the ticking of the human clock.

The black rock bounding my little bay had apparently been laid down as sediment about one and a half billion years ago. Some time later—500 million years, perhaps, or a billion—minerals infiltrated the rock's cracks and fissures. Appreciably later—about A.D. 1883—these minerals attracted one of those hairy malcontents whose vitality opens up every new world and keeps it spinning until better-adjusted individuals move in behind and do the dull but necessary job of organizing things. This particular pioneer was a twenty-five-year-old chronic wanderer from Indiana who during a spell as railroad conductor in New York City had contracted tuberculosis and had come out to the dry Southwest in a last desperate effort to find a cure. His name: William Wallace Bass.

The desert apparently did its job. Bass lived on. But he extracted no more money from copper and asbestos than did the fistful of other hardy prospectors in the Canyon. Then, as so often happens in the life of a man or a journey or an isolated community, events took an unexpected turn. To make frayed ends meet, William Bass began to guide hunting and prospecting parties—just as another miner, John Hance, was doing farther up the Canyon. And this venture prospered. Adjusting to the new state of affairs, Bass began to encourage tourists. On the Rim he built a rough-and-ready "dude ranch" and called it Bass Camp. He constructed a trail from this camp down through cliff and terrace and talus to the river and beyond. (I found the foundations of two stone cabins

on the rock platform above my camp.) Later he
stretched a stout wire cable across the Colorado. And
on this cable he ferried over the river, in a crude but
strong cable car, people and horses and whatever supplies he needed for his mining and his tourist parties.

Bass lived forty years in the Canyon. Until he re-
tired, at seventy-six, he continued to lead tourists
down from his camp to the Colorado. He died at
eighty-three, and his ashes were scattered on an im-
posing minaret of a butte called Holy Grail Temple
that towered four thousand feet above his cable.

William Bass built well. At Bass Camp at least one
house still stands. His trail, though no longer maintained, is still a freeway to a hiker. And although sixty
years have passed since he strung his cable across the
river, and perhaps forty since he last maintained it, I
stood on the creaking wooden platform of the still-
suspended cable car and felt no more than mildly nervous.

Bass had left other traces too. I reached my little
bay down a steep and narrow trail that I chanced to
stumble upon. The trail had been hewn out of the
black and twisted rock. Now plants were beginning to
reclaim its surface. And fragments of fallen rock half-
blocked my path. (Disturbed rock no longer operates
by the geologic clock; a considerable number of man-
loosened fragments may fall in a mere forty years.)
But the trail was still passable. As I eased my way
downward for the first time I wondered why Bass had
built it.

At its foot I found the answer. In the center of a
smooth, wind-created hollow there angled up from the
hot and glaring sand—almost too symbolic to be
true—the shaft of an ancient oar. The wood was gray
and cracked, and scoured by swirling water. The sun
beat down on it, and gusts of wind kept veiling it in

small and almost soundless sandstorms. Beyond the hollow, neatly stacked against black rock by flood-waters, I found a little pile of bleached wood and a rusty oarlock. Close by lay two cracked and splintered oar blades. One of them still had its protective metal end-band held in place by a single distorted rivet. These relics spoke eloquently. For I knew that until Bass built his cable system he had ferried men and supplies across the river in a long, puntlike rowboat. And even afterward he no doubt used the boat from time to time, when the cable stuck, or when a tourist balked at crossing in the decidedly airy cable car.

My little bay was full of other echoes too. Echoes of past and present. Every sound I made, even the rattle of cooking pots, came back to me across the river from the far wall of the Gorge, and I pictured William Bass living forty years with the echoes of his own actions in this corner of the Canyon he had made his own. When I clambered up a sidegully of the bay to inspect his cable I pictured him clambering up this same way on one of his earliest reconnaissances, before he built the trail. I saw him only as a wraith—the sort of faint wraith we all become; but I saw him, all right, clambering along just ahead of me. Barely eighty years ahead. And when I came back down the trail to my camp he was there again—only forty or fifty years ahead now—and walking a shade more stiffly as he led one of his cable-shy tourists down the well-kept trail to the little bay in which he beached his rowboat.

From what I had heard, the consensus of Grand Canyon opinion held William Bass to be no great shakes as a man. But in the short time I camped in his bay I felt that I came to know something about him. The part of him, I mean, that belonged to Grand Canyon.

It did not come to me at once, this grasp of what Bass and I shared. At first, when I wondered why he stayed on after it became clear that he was not going to make money from copper or asbestos, I found no adequate answer except "inertia." But by the second day I accepted without question that it was fascination with the Canyon. An affection, in particular, for those corners of it that he had made his own. It is something like this, I think, that most often keeps men in remote and unlikely places—whether they recognize it or not.

At first I by no means shared Bass's affection for his chosen corner. The first afternoon I camped in the bay dark clouds pressed down, heavy and somber. The twisted rocks pressed inward, black and oppressive. Gusts of wind swooped and snarled, rasping away with their gritty load. Except for the green river (down close, it looked green rather than blue-green), the place was almost as sullen and gloomy as the Gorge had been on my reconnaissance below Supai. But that evening the sun broke through and turned the black rock red and framed the hanging cable car in the arch of a Technicolor rainbow. Next day, in unbroken sunshine, I found that I understood why Bass had stayed on. Like me, he had sat in this bay and seen the sun strike red on distant cliff faces. Had watched the slanting light burnish first one black slab and then another into gleaming ebony. As the heat grew, he had heard and felt and welcomed the afternoon breezes. And after dark, in calm, cathedral beauty, he had sat and watched the rich black moon-shadow of the Gorge's rim move steadily out across the river.

On my second night in the bay, the moon shone so

brightly that although I sat in shadow I could see well enough to eat dinner. But when I looked out over the calm water I found that moonlight had blurred the temporary outline that time and chance erosion had imposed on the rocks. Instead, it illuminated their inner form: the parallel layers, twisted and contorted now by heat and pressure, in which they had been laid down as sediment on the bed of an ocean, one and a half billion years before. And I knew that William Bass, a prospector, would also have seen this X-ray effect of moonlight. Perhaps he had been moved to much the same thoughts about time and his present as I was thinking. It would be difficult not to think that way if you lived for long in such a place.

But there was one big difference between the bay I had camped in and the bay in which Bass had beached his rowboat. For me, the river was not only a source of reasonably clean drinking water, an inviting swimming pool, and an auxiliary larder, but also a thing of calm and silent beauty. In sunshine it sparkled. In moonlight it gleamed. And always it softened the harshness of black rock. When I first came down into the bay I had found myself for the first time in three weeks beside an expanse of water bigger than a rain-pocket, and as I knelt at the river's edge to fill my canteens I saw a ladybird floating on the calm green surface. The sight was as pleasing to my senses as is the year's first robin on a well-kept lawn.

But the river William Bass knew was the untamed Colorado—"too thick to drink, too thin to plow"—that during a heavy summer runoff might rage through its gorge forty feet higher than at low water. It was still the liquid grindstone that by sheer force of racing water and abrasive sand and pounding boulders had, when a huge dome rose in its path, adjusted to the new state of affairs by cutting through the center of that dome.

I found myself comparing the two rivers, Bass's and mine. Comparing them from the river's point of view.

As so often happens in the life of a river or a man or a journey or a community, events had just taken an unexpected turn. Ever since life appeared on earth it has been influencing the history of the earth's crust: shellfish live and die, live and die, live and die, and in time their empty shells build the Redwall; a tree root pries open a fissure, and in time another rock falls. But these have been slow, random, undirected influences. Then, quite recently, life produced conscious thought. Produced an intellect that is capable of at least some direction. And yesterday intellect devised dams.

It was by no means clear, when I stopped to think about it, how the river would respond to the new state of affairs just created by Glen Canyon Dam. Most likely, I decided, it would not really have to respond. For dams, though they look like rather permanent structures to us, seem certain to be very temporary impediments from the river's point of view. Long before the river reacts, our feeble dams will have crumbled.*

---

*From a short-term point of view I was quite wrong in deciding that the river would not have to respond. The changes brought about by Glen Canyon Dam—and certainly by other control measures now under consideration—would have immediate and radical effects on the whole delicately balanced mechanism of flood and drought, erosion and deposition, and fluctuating life zones. For example, flash floods often sweep huge masses of rock and rubble down sidecanyons and half-block the main river. Without regular floods to scour its channel the Colorado might soon degenerate into a chain of dead-water lakes.

But down at Bass's cable I was thinking of the river's long-term point of view. And there I was about right. The dams will have crumbled, all right, before the river needs to respond very much to any further raising of the dome that created the Canyon. They will certainly have vanished long before the Canyon flattens out—as it must do before so very long, geologic time—and in its own turn vanishes.

To me, camped in Bass's little bay, the river's point of view was almost as real as my own; but when you are thoroughly meshed with the outside world it is by no means easy to see things that way. Two days after I came

Meanwhile, "my" river flowed green and friendly.

It was the river's low level that encouraged me to make a one-day reconnaissance of the Gorge above Bass Trail, just as it had encouraged me to reconnoiter above Havasu Creek. As things turned out, the low level proved critical, for I had to make one short air-mattressing detour around an almost sheer rock buttress, and the slow-moving water made it an easy maneuver. With the river at normal level it would probably have been impossible to dog-paddle upriver around the point of that jutting buttress.

I would guess that my prime motive in making the reconnaissance was to explore for sheer satisfaction a stretch of country that it seemed likely no one had ever traveled over on foot; but I had a prosaic practical reason too. Once I struck eastward from Bass Trail along the Tonto Platform, I would have a long way to go before I came to the first water—half as far again as the distance from Fossil Bay to Apache Point. The going promised to be easier this time, and now my body was another week more tightly tuned. But I had decided to play safe: to back-pack water out for some distance and make a cache. So for the reconnaissance I striped my pack bag off its frame and in

---

out of the Canyon I visited Hoover Dam. Our guide solemnly announced in the course of his otherwise excellent patter that the dam was "built to last indefinitely." Afterward, on the side, I suggested that perhaps this remark was a little misleading. "Oh," he said, not really comprehending, "it was just that I didn't want to make it too complicated. People only get confused."

He had not, apparently, heard tell of Ozymandias, or considered that in the flicker of time since Hoover Dam was built in 1933 the Colorado has silted up the top forty miles of Lake Mead, the temporary reservoir created behind the dam.

Fresh from the Canyon, I found myself sadly unimpressed by Hoover Dam. All I could think of as the guide herded us through shining labyrinths of turbines and elevators was: "What a ball this is going to be for archeologists in three or four thousand years!" I tried the thought on one co-visitor, but drew a stony blank.

its place lashed the empty five-gallon can I had carried down from the Bass Camp cache.

The reconnaissance hit all its practical targets. I climbed carefully and laboriously, with only the one air-mattress detour, for almost five hours and barely two river-miles along the steep wall of the gorge. At the mouth of Serpentine Canyon I filled my five-gallon can from the river, added chlorinating tablets, and with water slap-slap-slapping metallically behind my shoulder blades found a way up the sidecanyon onto the Tonto Platform. I cached the water under an overhang, Butcharted back along the Platform and down the last thousand feet of Bass Trail, and reached camp at dusk with the comforting knowledge that next day I could climb slowly up to the Platform, amble a couple of hours along it, camp and rest in well-watered comfort, and then the following morning tackle a waterless stretch that had already been cut by 20 per cent.

But the day also hit higher targets. Even higher than my pleasantly self-indulgent aim of pioneering a probably virgin stretch of country. Quite by accident, it generated the first of the week's two catalysts.

In order to photograph a scene that for interest and balance demanded a figure in the foreground, I had mounted my camera on its lightweight collapsible tripod for a delayed-action self-portrait shot. But as I moved into position a gust of wind sent camera and tripod crashing over. And afterward the shutter refused to function.

I had brought only this one camera down into the Canyon, and at first I simmered with frustration. But within an hour I discovered a new fact of life. I recognized, quite clearly, that photography is not really compatible with contemplation. Its details are too insistent. They are always buzzing around your mind and clouding the fine focus of appreciation. You rarely detect this interference at the time, and cannot do much about it even if you do. But that morning of the Serpentine reconnaissance, after the camera had broken, I found myself freed from an impediment I had not known existed. I had escaped the tyranny of film. Now, when I came to something interesting, I no longer stopped, briefly, to photograph and forget; I stood and stared, fixing truer images on the emulsion of memory.

And the reconnaissance, set free, became a carnival—a bonus carnival, like one of the unexpected half-holidays we used to get at school for events quite beyond our control, such as the birth of yet another child to the headmaster's gratifyingly fecund wife. The carnival spirit carried me up the steep side-slopes of Serpentine Canyon and along the Tonto Trail. When I got back to camp it was still there. And it lasted to the end of my stay in William Bass's little bay. To the very end.

I left the bay for the last time soon after nine o'clock in the morning, and just before I did so there occurred a curious little incident that was in itself so ordinary, even potentially ugly, that I cannot quite explain how it became transformed into a kind of solemn yet joyous dedication of the place. I feel almost ashamed to use such high-sounding words; but I know that is the way I felt it.

I had carried my weekly bottle of claret down from the Bass Camp cache and had drunk the wine at my first riverside dinner. When the time came to leave I did not really like the idea of throwing the empty bottle into the river, but that seemed the safest and tidiest thing to do. To make sure it would sink, I filled it with water. I stood for a moment with the unstoppered bottle in my hand, feeling guilty at the thought of disturbing the green water that stretched across, calm and serene, to the blackness of the far rockwall. Then I leaned back, paused, and hurled the bottle with all my might out toward the middle of the river.

The bottle arched high above the green water, tumbling slowly, end over end. And as it swung up and over in the morning sunlight there Catherine-wheeled out from it a diamond-scattering of spray. This curved and sparkling arc of water seemed to hang suspended, as if time had slowed to a crawl. I stood watching, tense and breathless. And as the bottle tumbled slowly onward, still scattering diamonds into the sunshine, I was suddenly and acutely aware that something almost magical had taken over the scene. Everything I could see had an aura about it, an almost visible halo.

When the bottle began to swing downward at last, I think I half expected an arm to reach up from the water and grasp it and wave it three times before dragging it down and away forever. No arm appeared; but it did not really matter. For as the bottle landed it exploded a new fountain of spray. This new and beautiful shape crystallized the whole glistening, still-hanging pattern into a perfectly balanced unity. And that, for the long-drawn-out moment it lasted, was almost as good.

Such wild fancies of the mind rarely seem real in our sober, everyday world. So rarely, in fact, that I was at first reluctant to try putting it all down on paper. But I know, even now, that as I stood watching the last of the spray float gently down, waiting for calm to return slowly to that calm place, it seemed as though I had performed a kind of dedication. A dedication and a fitting farewell.

An hour later I had climbed a thousand feet up Bass

Trail onto the Tonto Platform. As I turned eastward I stopped and looked back down Bass Canyon toward the place, hidden now, where fifty-five years earlier a young malcontent from Indiana had strung his cable across the river. I looked in particular for the little sandy bay in which he had beached his rowboat. And—not quite knowing whether I meant man or place, but feeling it was more likely the place—I said: "Good-bye, Bass." I said it out loud, to the space and the silence; and I said it with affection. And when I walked on eastward I found myself comparing, with a surprise that bordered on astonishment, the oppression I had felt when I first went down to the sandy bay, three days earlier, with the warm affection that now filled me.*

When you look down onto the Tonto Platform from the Rim of Grand Canyon you see a flat gray rock terrace that hangs on the very lip of the Inner Gorge. It seems to be quite bare and looks like a very dull place indeed.

When you walk along the Tonto Trail (which runs the whole length of the Tonto Platform and is nowadays, like the Apache Trail, really a wild burro trail) you find that the grayness you saw from above came not from rock but from sparse, dowdy, knee-high

*I need not have been surprised. Other people have found that the Canyon takes some getting used to. And for me this somber section of the Inner Gorge was something new, standing apart.

In 1882, Clarence E. Dutton wrote: "The lover of nature whose perceptions have been trained elsewhere will enter this strange region with a shock, and dwell there for a time with a sense of oppression. The bold will seem grotesque, the colors too bizarre, the subtlety absent. But time will bring a gradual change, and the strength and majesty will come through. Great innovations, whether in art or literature, in science or in nature, seldom take the world by storm. They must be understood before they can be estimated, and they must be cultivated before they can be understood."

bushes. This scraggy fleece part-covers a coarse and often stony soil that varies in color from pale green through gray to almost purple, according to which layers of the many-hued Tonto shale and slate lie close to the surface. And the Platform turns out to be by no means as flat as you had imagined. Even when you swing around a ridge or butte onto the prominent spurs, or headlands, that were all you really saw of the terrace from the Rim, you are always climbing a slope or easing down its far side. You spend less time out on these spurs than you do in sidecanyons, for the sidecanyons cut back much more deeply than you had imagined. And in these canyons the going is rough.

You are in for another mild surprise too. Although the Platform hangs on the lip of the Gorge, the Tonto Trail tends to hug the inner talus, and you rarely see the Colorado. Occasionally you hear the faint roar of rapids. If you walk to the edge of the Platform, there is the river, a thousand feet below, at the foot of its plunging black walls. But if you keep to the trail you find yourself walking quite alone, in a world cut off from everything above and below.

Away to the left cuts the black chasm of the Inner Gorge. It is a barrier to more than your body. Because of it, the cliffs and terraces beyond are not a part of your world. You look at them, of course, may even take time to study a particular feature; but mostly (if your mind works the way mine does) everything on the far side of the Gorge moves past as if it existed behind a huge pane of glass.

To your right towers the Redwall. Sometimes you walk close and can pick out a small gray patch where a rock fragment peeled away so recently that iron oxide from the terrace above has not yet had time to seep down and restain the newly exposed surface. Sometimes the trail swings wide, and your eye, encompassing mile after mile of smooth red cliff face, can savor the sweep of each bay and promontory. The Rim, when you can see it, hangs high above and far, far back. The world beyond it lies somewhere out beyond the horizons of your imagination.

When I began to walk through this curiously segregated world I think I was afraid that it would turn out to be as dull as it had looked from the Rim. I need not have worried. The film-free carnival mood came with me. Even, I think, something of the Excalibur mood from William Bass's little bay. And the Tonto Platform responded.

All through the first afternoon I rested beneath the overhang in which I had cached my five gallons of water. Even during the heat of the day it was cool and relaxing there, deep in the shadow of the rock. A bush that by some quirk of chance had germinated far back in a crack in the roof had been forced to grow downward and then outward to meet the light, and a bird's nest neatly woven into its overhanging branches gave the place a comfortable kind of under-the-eaves-of-my-country-cottage feeling. After dark I stood my flashlight on its base and a white alkali-stain on the roof reflected a soft and efficient glow. I slept lightly, the way I tend to if I know that I need an early start next day; and when, soon after four o'clock, I looked out of my picture doorway I saw the morning star slide up over the North Rim. During breakfast, as the night began to slip away, I heard an owl calling me to harness from somewhere high in the emerging Redwall; and by the time I had swung halfway around the first spur sunlight came flooding over the buttes like the incoming tide.

All morning I hurried eastward, halting only for brief hourly rests. Spur, sidecanyon, spur, then sidecanyon again. Sometimes the spur-to-spur cycle took an hour, sometimes two; but always there was a steady, rhythmic inevitability about it, comforting and compelling. So compelling that I did not stop for lunch until almost two o'clock. But when I did so at last I knew that I had broken the back of the first long, waterless stretch of the Tonto Platform. And after that the day was different.

But the change stemmed from more than assurance of success. For this was the day I introduced, again more or less accidentally, the week's second catalyst.

Walkers and mountaineers and the like can be divided into two distinct breeds: those who put on the clothes they think are about right, and then stick it out, hour after hour, without apparent discomfort; and those who peel and restore in response to every variation of effort and environment. I belong to the thermally responsive faction: it takes hardly a mile of walking or a side glance of sunshine to strip me down to hat, socks, boots, underpants, and shorts. This was the way I had traveled almost every day since Fossil Bay. But now I had moved not only well into May but also deeper into the Canyon—down to barely three thousand feet above sea level. At noon the day before, in welcome shade, my thermometer had registered 86 degrees. Out in the sun, on bare sand, it had been 126 degrees—and of course I could almost never walk in the shade. But the human body is a remarkably adaptable piece of machinery, and as long as a breeze was blowing I rarely felt too uncomfortable. When the breeze died, though, the heat clamped down.

At lunchtime on the day beyond my five-gallon overhang, the breeze suddenly died. The heat clamped. All at once it occurred to me that in the privacy of the Canyon I could carry my thermostatic clothing system to its logical conclusion. And I promptly stripped to hat, socks, and boots.

Now, nakedness is a delightful condition. And it keeps you very pleasantly cool—especially, I suppose, if you happen to be a man. But as I walked on eastward that afternoon through my private, segregated, Tonto world (exercising due care at first for previously protected sectors of my anatomy) I found I had gained more than coolness. I felt a quite unexpected sense of freedom from restraint. And after a while I found that I had moved on to a new kind of simplicity. A simplicity that had a fitting, Adam-like, in-the-beginning earliness about it.

The new simplicity was there, working, all that afternoon, and all through the days that followed.

Freed from the pressure of haste, the tyranny of film, and now the restraint of clothes, I found myself looking more closely at what went on around me. Not only at a network of white dikes that reached up and out into the black walls of the Inner Gorge, like huge varicose veins serving the molten heart of the earth. Not only at caves hanging high and inaccessible on the Redwall, fascinating as fairy castles can be in childhood. But at the close-ups. At the minutiae. At the network of life that spreads, almost invisible, across the Spartan and apparently inhospitable expanse of the Tonto Platform.

At first I saw only things. Intriguing and often beautiful things, but still just single, unconnected, three-dimensional items.

A prickly pear blazed purple on bare talus. An agave stalk thrust up twenty feet of clustered yellow blooms, and bumblebees droned ponderously around the flowers' entrances, pollen sacs yellow and pendulous. I stopped for lunch, and ants arrived to remove the crumbs: big ants carrying big loads, small ants carrying stupendous loads.

Once, resting in the cool of an overhang, I watched

a translucent brown insect scrambling over the stones toward me. It was about half an inch long, six-legged, twin-antennaed, and needle-headed. The upper surface of its body was flat, with cupped edges that made the creature look like a tiny, shallow, pedestrian bowl. I watched for a while as it scrambled nearer. It moved with considerable agility. And some fixed, insatiable purpose seemed to drive it on. Lazily, I wondered why it had such an oddly shaped body. Then my mind meandered off.

A few minutes later I noticed another insect crossing the stones, in the opposite direction. This one, though about the same length, was an ungainly creature, hardly able to haul its heavy, bulbous body along. It moved lethargically, quite without the driving intent of the first. But it too, I noticed, had six legs. And two antennae. An a needle-sharp head. The head looked vaguely familiar, and I bent closer. Then I looked at the body again. It was round and distended, but there was something familiar about that too. And then I saw that the body was distended with a dark-red liquid. And all at once I knew that the liquid was warm as well as red. Was warm mammalian blood. Welsh blood. My blood.

Noon on the trail. I stopped in midstride: three feet from my boots lay a lizard. Cameraless, I crouched slowly down until my eyes were within nine inches of the fat and panting body. The lizard basked on. I took notes. On the roof of the solemn, philosophical, brown-gray head bulged two domes, one above each eye, like a pair of slightly compressed igloos. Around the neck ran a startling collar of blue-gray and white stripes. Back and flanks were speckled; the athletically slim legs, dappled; the long, artistic fingers of the feet, front and rear, a warm golden-brown; and the tail, tapering away almost endlessly, as if reluctant to give way to mere empty space, a uniform and magnificent gold. For a long time the lizard basked on, panting, eyes staring directly ahead in their slightly glazed, reptilinear way. Then, for no apparent reason, it darted off into a patch of scrub.

It was early morning, the day's freshness untarnished. The rattlesnake lay beside the trail, belly up, head pounded almost to pulp, stomach and part of one flank already eaten away by some small-jawed animal. I turned I over. The back was distinctly pink. I stretched the corpse out. It measured a shade over three feet. It was not yet stiff. I examined the scuffle of footprints in the dust and saw that its executioners had been wild burros.*

I had been in wild-burro country ever since I crossed the precipitous head of Forster Canyon, back on the far side of Apache Point. The burros came in two brands: buff with black shoulder-and-back stripes, and plain chocolate. All had grizzled muzzles. By effectively maintaining the Tonto Trail through sheer footwork, they seemed to me to have established ownership of the Tonto Platform. Thanks to them there was always—hour after hour, day after day—at least one trail for me to follow.

Often, in fact, the burros had created not one trail but a network. There was usually no doubt about which branch to follow, but sometimes I erred along one created by an obstinate right-wing minority group that liked to wander up the talus toward the Redwall. This let's-go-up-the-hill faction always recognized its mistake in the end and rejoined the main assembly,

---

*Herpetologists classify these pink Grand Canyon rattlesnakes as a distinct subspecies of the prairie rattler *(Crotalus viridis)*. And they have given them the pleasingly apt name *abyssus*. Its cousin-neighbor on the South Rim, used by Hopi Indians as a symbolic messenger to the gods in their famous annual snake dance, is labeled, just as pleasingly, *nuntius*, or "messenger."

but to judge by their readiness to deviate again they remained unrepentant. Occasionally a whole web of trails converged at a rolled-bare dust bath. Once, where the soil reflected the junction of contrasting Tonto shales, I was offered and declined two such baths, one purple-red and one green.

There were other reminders of the burros too. Several times a day I would hear, somewhere out in the space and silence, a selection from their wide repertoire of lifelike imitations, ranging from the snort of a dyspeptic colonel to the lowing of a locomotive. And occasionally I would surprise one of them browsing among the green bushes and cottonwood trees that grew on the floors of most sidecanyons, or I would meet one standing with hang-burro mien out in the blazing sun.

Such meetings, like my meetings with the rattle-snake and the lizard and the blood-bibbing insect, were at first no more than meetings. No more than the chance intersection of two animals' life-paths.

But after two days of carnival and rhythmic progress along the Platform—spur and sidecanyon, spur and sidecanyon, sunrise and noon and sunset, silence and space and solitude, Gorge and Redwall and distant Rim, sunrise and sunset, spur and sidecanyon—I found myself beginning to see beyond the meetings. I found myself seeing us all not merely as animals that happened to be there on the Platform, but as passing performers in a long, long dance. And I found that I understood this dance not merely with the thin comprehension of intellect, but so radically and so clearly that after a little while its surge and rhythm were as sure as the meetings themselves, if not surer.

I saw the burros now as recent accidental importations by such men as William Bass. I saw them as creatures that had found in the Canyon, and in particular along the Tonto Platform, an empty or sparsely occupied niche in which they could live and thrive and multiply, even in the face of a stupidly conceived Park policy that at one time sought to eliminate them. I saw them too as the hosts that, above all, made it possible for small insects with shallow blood-bowls on their backs to fill those bowls often enough to keep alive. (It was not often, obviously, that these insects smelled, Fee, Fi, Fo, Fum, the blood of a hot Welsh-man.)

And I began to see—clearly, in my confused Celtic way—other linkages. I saw the burros as execution-ers with frenzied hooves that played a minor part in keeping within reasonable bounds the population of pink-backed rattlesnakes. I saw the rattlesnakes as organisms that were in part kept alive by—and also helped keep under control—speckled Western col-lared lizards that basked in the sun, plump and pant-ing, in order to warm their cold, premammalian blood sufficiently to hunt, or even to digest their hunted food. I saw the lizard as an organism that in part kept itself alive by feeding on small insects that in their turn kept themselves alive by feeding on warm-blooded burros. I saw the lizard too, feeding on other insects that buzzed, busy in bright desert sunlight, around the entrances of yellow flowers clustering on a Maypole-straight agave stalk.

And I saw the agave now as a part of the green bedrock of life on earth. As a part of the plant life that captures for this planet the energy of the sun and stores this energy and hands it on to insects that buzz around its yellow flowers sucking nectar, and to other animals that feed on other parts of it, such as certain kinds of lizards, or perhaps a browsing wild burro, or a party of Supai Indians squatting around a mescal pit. A burro or an Indian that in turn gives nourishment to a blood-bowl of an insect that in turn feeds a lizard that in turn feeds a rattlesnake that in turn feeds something else with small jaws . . .

In other words, as I walked on eastward along the Tonto Platform, almost as naked as the other animals, I began to see everything around me as an intricate, interlocking web of life.

And the web, I saw, covered more than the three dimensions of the Tonto Platform. It also extended back in time.

I saw in the pinkness of the rattlesnake the result of an immensely slow but very sure selection that had taken place during the comparatively recent two or three million years since the Canyon began to approach its present size. A selection favoring individuals that by chance were born pink. For because their color blended with the dominant pink of the Canyon's rock and so protected them from enemies, these pink individuals tended to escape the attention of their enemies more often, and so to live longer than their neighbors, and so to produce more offspring—which in turn tended more and more often to have pink skins.

Now I saw the lizard not just as an individual organism, but as a life that was helping to carry forward the development of a species that had in its time helped carry forward the development of life from cold-blooded to warm-blooded land animals. I saw it as a twig on a branch of life that may still, for all we mammals know, have a viable future.

I saw that such single-minded creatures as little walking blood-bowls (which presumably fed on nothing but their favorite food) could hardly have prospered until warm-blooded mammals such as ground squirrels or wild burros or stray Welshmen had already gained a footing.

And I saw the flowering agave as a newcomer form of plant life. For brightly colored flowers would not have evolved successfully if there had been no insects for their bright colors to attract. (Individual plants that by chance mutation produced flowers would have gained no advantage for their kind: they would not at that time have attracted insects. Not, at least, insects that could act as unknowing agents for the spread of the plants' reproductive pollen—and thereby increase the number of these plants' progeny so effectively that in the end the newfangled flower bearers would compete out of existence those similar plants that had not happened to produce flowers.) Now, there have probably been plants on the land surface of the earth for something like 400 million years—that is, since soon after the laying-down of the mud that is now the shale of the Tonto Platform. But flying insects of the kind likely to cross-pollinate flowers regularly in the course of their own search for nectar did not appear in large numbers until about 180 million years ago—that is, after the creation of the white limestone of the Canyon's present Rim. Soon afterward (10 million years later, say, or 30 million), flowering plants duly began to flourish. They are, as I say, comparative newcomers in the plant world.

But perhaps I am cheating when, in an effort to convey how things looked to me during those hot and rhythmic days along the Tonto Platform, I quote these specific biological details. I rather doubt that during those days I fully understood them all. Yet, oddly enough, it does not matter. For I do not believe that at the time I *thought* very much about this intricate web-in-time: I *felt* it. Felt myself an integral part of everything that went on around me. Felt it with a simple and straightforward certainty I had never known before. Felt myself not only as a part of the web of life as it happened to exist in the present, but as a part of the throbbing, pulsating process that is all we know. A process of which this present web is merely a fingerprint.

As I walked on eastward, spur after spur after side-canyon, day after day, I think I must have known that the time had not yet come to look too closely at this web. For although the animal meetings were perhaps the highlight events of each day, what occupied my eyes and my mind more steadily—minute after minute, hour after hour, spur after sidecanyon—were still the rocks, that foundation across which the web of life is spread and from which it almost certainly arose.

Yet the web was always there now. It was certainly there at Boucher Creek.

It was noon, and I was hot and tired and ready for lunch. The Tonto Trail cut back half a mile into yet another sidecanyon, then angled steeply down a hundred feet into a harsh and ovenlike landscape. In front of me two ravines converged. Nowhere could I see a sign of the water I had expected. I trudged on up the easterly ravine. The map called it Boucher Creek. No breeze penetrated that sunken place. The heat pressed down on me, as if suddenly in league with gravity. My pack sagged. And then, all at once, a thread of clear water was sparkling on bare rock. I walked on up beside it with light and springing step. The thread broadened. Half a mile, and I camped in the shade of some green creekside bushes. Soon I was stretched out cool and naked on my sleeping bag.

The little creek, still less than a foot wide, bubbled and babbled past so close that I could reach out whenever I wanted to and scoop up a cupful of cool drinking water. All I could see was green foliage and a hint of glaring rock beyond. That, and the sparkling creek and the oddly humped, blue-gray rock over which it flowed. All I could hear was the tinkle of the creek and the lazy hum of insects and, once, the trumpeting of a distant burro.

Stretched out on my sleeping bag in the shade of the bushes, I half dozed the rest of the day away (for I knew now that, barring accidents, I would reach Phantom Ranch quite comfortably before my food ran out). And as the hours passed I found that I had become, almost physically, a part of the green and shady little world that was for the moment all I knew. Slowly, the way it always happens, I began to piece together the relationships of the place: the big half-buried boulder that had created a kink in the creek; the stone over which the creek had cascaded and formed a pool that apparently meant home to at least one toad; and a bare streamside patch of gravel so low-lying that it was half-awash and rimmed with white alkali stain from the creek water.

Several hours passed, I think, before I really thought about the raised and oddly humped blue-gray rock along which the creek ran. It was certainly some time before I realized that the alkaline water of the creek had built it, just as Havasu Creek had built its own travertine falls.

Soon, lying there beside the creek, almost physically a part of it now, I found myself trying to look at the place through the eyes of the other organisms that used it. Through the eyes of the burro whose trumpeted complaint I had heard, and the eyes of the toad that sat basking on the rim of its swimming-pool home, and even through the eyes of the insects whose lazy recitative made the bushes an open-air opera house. I saw that to all these animals—and especially to the insects, because they lived and died by the thousands in a span that was short even by human standards—the creek would inevitably seem changeless. Not for them, certainly, the slow buildup of the gray-blue rock, raising the creek millimeter by millimeter above the surrounding land and flooding the patch of gravel. Not for most of them, even, the huge changes that came every few years with flash floods of the sort that would in time carry away the half-buried boulder that had created the kink in the creek. Yet such changes are quite obvious to us humans, even when we are embedded in a clanking civilization that drowns out the more deliberate rhythms. The changes are obvious not so much because we are longer-lived—though that is a part of it—but because we have for some time been tinged with a revolutionary but still rudimentary mode of operating which we call logical thought; and also because we record happenings and even concepts in written symbols and so hand down knowledge from generation to generation (a useful product of our logic that we have employed for several years now; about five thousand, anyway).

After a while, as I lay there beside the creek, naked and passive, the band of raised blue-gray rock seemed to be growing so fast that I almost expected to see its outline change. Yet I had already accepted that the droning insects and the basking toad must see the rock as "everlasting hills." And it was then that I understood, with a clarity I had never known before, the smallness of our human time scale. Understood what is obvious enough, really: that the longest time spans we fully accept in our everyday lives are far shorter compared with the stately eons of the rock than are the time spans of the insects compared with our own.

That lazy afternoon beside the blue-gray rockbed of Boucher Creek once more carried my journey forward. For afterward I found myself understanding the story of the rocks in a way I had not done even on the

day I walked down Bass Trail. Found myself understanding not just words and paragraphs but something of the plot as well—the way the chapters fitted
together, flowing through time. Found myself understanding this flow more certainly and more steadily,
without break or effort. Understanding that the story
was still being written and that I was walking through
it. Had always been walking through it.

And I began to assimilate at last the lessons that
the Canyon had, all along, been laying out for me to
read. Some of them were kindergarten lessons, so
scaled down that they could fall comfortably within
our everyday horizons.

One such simple lesson from three weeks earlier
now clicked into delayed and unexpected focus. I saw
once more the toadstool rock that I had stopped to
photograph on the Esplanade—a rock exactly like a
huge red-brown toadstool, ten feet high, cut away at
its base almost to toppling-point and flaring out to a
massive round banqueting-table of a top. But now, instead of a spectacular oddity, a random photogenic
freak, I saw a proof of the blasting power of sand
blown close to the ground, century after century—the
same sand that collected thick and red in my cooking
pots when I left them uncovered. The static toadstool
rock became, in other words, a living lesson. The solid
proof of a geologic process. A proof that had itself
been changing as it moved forward in time even while
I stood and photographed it.

And it was the same when I left Boucher Creek and
walked on eastward again along the Tonto Platform.

Early next morning I came to Travertine Creek and
saw, sure enough, great convoluted slabs of red-brown
travertine rock crisscrossing its ravine. The place was
dry as a dust bowl; but it was a simple matter now
for me to picture a blue-green creek tumbling down

toward the Inner Gorge, just the way Havasu Creek still tumbled. In its time, this creek too had built convoluted, porcelain-white swimming pools. Then, through some chance flux of geology or climate, the creek had vanished and the white swimming pools had oxidized into bone-dry, red-brown slabs.

And when I crossed Monument Creek later that same day and saw the hundred-foot pillar that gave the creek its name, I recognized at once not just a freak but a passing freak. I knew without the need of technical knowledge that this pillar could hardly have separated from the wall of the sidecanyon very long before mankind was born. I knew that it could not last long either: it would topple any millennium now.

These were all easy understandings, of course. Short-term affairs. But it was the same now when I looked up at the smooth and curving faces of the Redwall and at the buttes and mesas and minarets towering above them. That hot afternoon at Boucher Creek, down among the humming insects, had dissolved the solidity of the "everlasting hills." They too represented a mere passing phase, changing at that very moment, in a process that nothing can alter.

And it was the same when I looked at the raw material from which this sculpture had been hewn. I saw, even more vividly than I had as I walked down Bass Trail, not just the rock but the building of it. I saw it more accurately too.

The day I walked down Bass Trail there had been one chapter in the Canyon's autobiography that had eluded me. Before coming down into the Canyon I had read about what the geologists call "The Great Unconformity." There was, it seemed, a large gap in time between two layers of rocks. Although the words had stuck in my mind, they had conveyed so little that I had not even registered clearly where the gap occurred. But as I moved toward the end of my four days' walk along the Tonto Platform I began to understand this Great Unconformity. To accept it not as a mere intellectual conjecture too immense and appalling to have much real meaning, but as a plain, incontrovertible fact. A fact I could see, now that my eyes were open, every time I looked at the Inner Gorge.

For all along the rim of the Gorge, the black and twisted rocks that rise steeply from the river come to an abrupt end. A horizontal line cuts across the agonized folding of the schists; and laid neatly along this line, like a huge, flat crust on a black, half-eaten pie, lies a slab of uniform brown sandstone. This Tapeats sandstone, two hundred feet thick, runs in an even and almost unbroken line along sixty miles of the Inner Gorge. The day I walked down Bass Trail through layer after layer of rock, I had instinctively seen the Tapeats as a mature but comparatively unworried rock. And instinct had been right: this sandstone had not yet been subjected to the terrible weight of time that had twisted and contorted the schists beneath. Below the sandstone I had seemed to step down into a different world. And instinct had again recorded accurately: between the creation of the schists and the creation of the sandstone there had elapsed a period of 500 million years.

Now, I cannot pretend that 500 million years meant very much to me yet. Not as a finite interval of time. But as I walked day after day along the Platform, with the brown piecrust of the Tapeats sandstone always lying there, blatantly, along the far rim of the Gorge, I came to feel the reality of what had happened.

A lot had happened in those 500 million years. The schists that are all you can see today in the Inner Gorge are the roots of ancient mountains that were once as tall, geologists say, as our present Alps. And during those 500 million years these mountains died. They were worn down—boulder by falling boulder, grain by wind-scoured grain, molecule by rain-dissolved molecule—until their surface was flat and even. Then new rocks (still visible in certain parts of the Canyon) were laid down on this surface, and then were raised up as new mountains, and then in their turn were worn away, until the flat and even surface of the old rock was once more exposed. Five hundred million years. And then, by chance, this level plain sank slowly beneath a shallow sea. Quite quickly, in a million or so years, perhaps, the sea covered it with light-brown sand. Covered it to a depth of two hundred feet. And then chance once more altered the face of the earth, so that there began to be deposited on that offshore sea bed not clean and granular sand but thick, soft mud from a river. Mud that was sometimes purple and sometimes green, according to what soil the river chanced to be eroding, far back up its course, at any given period. And in due time this mud became the purple and green shale that now forms the Tonto Platform. Meanwhile, pressure and water and the passage of time had cemented the buried sand into sandstone. Into a brown and uniform sandstone that spoke eloquently, now that I knew how to listen, of the gulf of time that yawned between it and the twisted black rock on which it rested. Spoke clearly of 500 million years.

Presently, it occurred to me that I had a scale for measuring those 500 million years. A scale independent of numbers. For it so happened that 500 million years was also the time that had elapsed between the creation of the piecrust Tapeats sandstone and my journey through Grand Canyon. And all I had to do to see what had happened in *those* 500 million years was to look up and around. I could see the purple and green of the Bright Angel shale. I could see above it the six hundred feet of Redwall that had been built up by the life and death and sinking down of tiny shellfish to the floor of some later ocean. Could see, higher again, the red layer of interleaved shale and sandstone, almost a thousand feet thick, that I had followed along the Esplanade, around Fossil Bay, and on to Bass Trail. Could see, yet higher, the brown, wind-blown sandstone that had once been desert sand dunes: the sandstone I had passed through below Hualpai Hilltop; the sandstone from which had been carved the little grotto beside the Bass Trail. And capping all these I could see the white limestone cliff that formed the Rim.

But that, I knew, was only half of it. Almost exactly half. The white limestone of the Rim had been created more than 200 million years ago. That is, only halfway through the span of time that had elapsed since the formation of the Tapeats sandstone. But the rocks had not always stopped there. Other layers had been built above them—and in the due course of time had been ground down by wind and water until they had vanished, almost as if they had never existed. And after all this had happened—in the last little seven-million-year flicker of a nod—the Colorado had created Grand Canyon.*

---

*Those upper layers have vanished *almost* as if they had never existed.
  Within a few miles of the South Rim of Grand Canyon stand two isolated and widely separated hills called Red Butte and Cedar Mountain. These hills, rising up from the same white limestone as forms the Canyon's Rim, are composed for the most part of clearly stratified red sandstones and shales. Almost identical rocks are still found throughout large areas to the north and east of Grand Canyon, and it seems certain that they once formed a continuous layer over the whole region. Then local conditions must have changed, just long enough for wind and water to erase this topmost layer. The fragmentary but persuasive evidence that it once existed has been left behind at Red Butte and Cedar Mountain by sheer chance: because the soft red rocks that now form Red Butte were protected from erosion by a layer

Other things had been happening too, all through those 500 million years. Events that my mind could attempt to measure on yet a different scale.

At the time the grains of sand that built the Tapeats sandstone were accumulating along their ancient seashore, the most complicated form of life on earth seems to have been a small sea creature called a trilobite, now extinct, whose fossil remains suggest to our eyes an overgrown sow bug or a small and simplified horseshoe crab. Trilobites were so far ahead of their time (so much more efficient at existing, that is, than were their competitors for existence) that it seems from fossil records as if they dominated the oceans of the world in both size and numbers. In the next 500 million years these trilobites evolved, without becoming any larger or much more complicated, into land-pioneering scorpions and nectar-transporting and blood-bibbing insects. But other forms of life which at that time were much simpler and less developed evolved, along different branches, into fish and frogs and toads and lizards and rattlesnakes and hummingbirds and ground squirrels and wild burros and men who built dams and cities and occasionally found it necessary or advisable or perhaps obscurely unavoidable to lift packs onto their backs and walk out and away from their cities.

All this succession of events I could see quite clearly as I walked along the Tonto Platform and looked at the Great Unconformity that so clearly existed between the black, contorted schists of the Inner Gorge and the uniform brown piecrust of the Tapeats sandstone. And although these events taught me nothing mathematical about the meaning of "500 million

---

of hard lava, and those of Cedar Mountain by pebble-rock. Today, these protective layers still cap the hills.

years," they provided a kind of touchstone against which I could feel the vast dimension of such an interval and could begin to assess it, meaningfully, in terms of the history of the earth.

This new touchstone opened my eyes and ears and mind to something that is obvious enough, really, though I suspect that most of us do not see and hear and understand it as clearly and as steadily as we should. Naked and free on the Tonto Platform I heard and understood and accepted with my whole being what I had begun to hear and understand at the foot of Bass Trail. I accepted, totally, that the world of the rocks, like all the other world we know, is dynamic. For now its rhythm was as real to me as the regular beat of the seconds that ticked past on my wrist watch. In fact, when I stopped to consider the matter, I discovered to my surprise that its rhythm was for the moment more real to me than the rhythm of the civilization that was presumably still going on in the world beyond the Rim.

The rhythm of the rocks beats very slowly, that is all. The minute hand of its clock moves by the millions of years. But it moves. And its second hand moves by the ceaseless eroding drip of a seep spring, by the stinging flight of sand particles on a gray and windy evening, by the particle-on-particle accretion of white travertine in warm blue-green waters—by the same ticking seconds that our watches record. And if you listen carefully—when you have immersed yourself long enough, physically and mentally, in enough space and enough silence and enough solitude—you begin to detect, even though you are not looking for it, something faintly familiar about the rhythm. You remember hearing that beat before, point and counterpoint, pulsing through the inevitable forward movement of river and journey, of species and isolated Indian community, of lizard and of flowering plant and of hairy malcontent from Indiana. And you grasp at last, in a fuller and more certain way than you ever have before, that all these worlds move forward, each at its own tempo, in harmony with some unique basic rhythm of the universe.*

The day before I reached Phantom Ranch, signs of man began to appear. Hermit Camp was a derelict dude ranch dry-rotting back into the desert. Just beyond it I passed the first Park Service sign I had seen since Supai. Soon, more fossils-in-the-making: a length of frayed and sun-bleached rope, a horseshoe, a rusty iron stove peacefully disintegrating. Before long, even a telephone line swinging incongruously down toward Indian Garden (where the Havasupai in their vital days seem to have encamped occasionally, and where the Tonto Trail crosses the busy tourist trail that runs from the Rim to Phantom Ranch).

Now, when I looked up at the Rim, I knew in some disjointed and rather tenuous sense that a hardtop road ran along its lip. Up there, I half accepted, tourists were stepping out of their cars to have their minds exploded beyond old boundaries by their first sight of the Canyon—or to glance at the view and then check their watches to see if the hotel had begun to serve lunch yet.

---

*Do not dismiss "some unique basic rhythm of the universe" as the mouthings of a dreamer too long divorced from "reality." I have lifted the phrase, gratefully, from the treatise of a hard-headed mathematician (G. J. Whitrow: *The Natural Philosophy of Time* [1961]). I read the book after I returned from my Canyon journey; but this accurate phrase, intellectually arrived at, conveys exactly what I felt in my confused way during those hot, rhythmic days during which I walked, innocent of camera and clothes, steadily eastward through my silent and private world of the Tonto Platform.

A couple more hours and I was walking—partly clothed now, and resenting it—through tourist-trampled dust. Next, a crumpled Hershey bar wrapper. Then, as I came in sight of the green foliage of Indian Gardens, the whine of a powerhouse. Finally, a man sitting on a stone, taking off his boots.

I followed the broad and dusty mule trail down to the Colorado and crossed a suspension bridge. And that evening I dined at a table, off plates, and chatted with other visitors to Phantom Ranch—the only tourist resort still operating in the Canyon, the only surviving remnant of a process that a hairy malcontent from Indiana had set in motion seventy years before when he led the first party of tourists down his trail to the waiting cable car or ferried them across the river from the quiet little bay in which he had beached his rowboat.

LIFE

—

I SHOULD have known, of course, that Phantom Ranch would drag me back into the present.

Most people go down to that quiet and secluded place directly from the world beyond the Rim and are therefore almost sure to see it as a sanctuary. An urbane and attractive blonde from New York whom I talked to soon after I arrived said in a hushed voice: "This is really the end of the line, isn't it?" But for me, inevitably, the ranch was padded civilization: fresh food, electricity, swimming pool, conversation, mail, typewriter—even a telephone. And on typewriter and telephone I found myself wrestling with just the kind of administrative detail that clutters up our everyday lives. So all through the week I stayed at the ranch I lived a curiously in-between existence. And when I walked out once more into the Canyon (I realized afterward that I did not quite think of Phantom as being "in" the Canyon) it was not the same.

The Canyon had not changed of course. At first I still walked along the Tonto Platform, with the Redwall and the Inner Gorge marking off my private, segregated world. I still walked naked, in space and silence and solitude. The sun still beat down, hotter every day.

And the beauty was still there too. Rock patterns hung like abstract paintings in open, sunlit galleries. A deer bounded away across the Platform, moving for one perfect moment in unison with racing cloud shadows. A hummingbird mistook my orange sleeping bag for a mammoth flower and with its stiletto of a beak probed daintily in the folds for nectar. But such scenes were static now. A series of unrelated stills. I no longer saw them as links in a complex chain that reached back and down into the roots of time.

And as I walked I no longer felt the pulse of the Canyon's longest rhythms. Brown Tapeats sandstone still stretched, mile after mile, along the rim of the Gorge. But I heard no real meaning behind the "500 million years" that intellect still told me divided it from the black schists below. The rock remained a piecrust oddity. Early one morning I found beside the Tonto Trail a slab of purple shale encrusted with wormlike fossil forms. They stood out vividly, as raised and writhing as if Michelangelo had carved them. But I received no ancient message. The slab remained a mere item for the storehouse of intellect. I photographed it, then moved on.

The photography, I suppose, built a barrier of its own. One of the administrative chores that cluttered my week at Phantom had been arranging for a new camera to be rushed by air from San Francisco to the Rim, then by mule down to the ranch. And now, as if to make up for the lost days between Bass and Phantom, the camera rode me more tyrannically than ever.

There were other barriers too. I found that during the week of civilized living I had slipped a notch or two out of my automatic wilderness routines. And now I faced a fresh physical challenge. In the first day and a half beyond Phantom I expected to find no water. Three or four days out, when the Tonto Platform tapered abruptly away, I would run into rough country. And on the eighth day I had another airdrop deadline to meet. So at first I found that, as had happened along the Esplanade, I spent much of my time asking and answering a stream of screwed-tight-to-the-minute questions: "How many hours left now to Grapevine Creek?" "Is the water going to last out?" "Am I really running low on dried milk?" "If that stretch along the river won't 'go,' can I still make the airdrop in time?"

But I must not suggest that the present clamped as tightly as it had along the Esplanade. For one thing, I had been walking for a month. When Harvey Butchart made a special trip down to Phantom to brief me on the remainder of the route he took one look at my midriff, grinned, and said: "Why, you've lost a good twenty pounds already." And my honed and hardened fitness meant that I was no longer harassed by many of the trivial but insistent details that had consumed the early days. Beyond Phantom, for example, the only time I used the once-precious Moleskins was as a pad to shim up a loose fitting between tripod and new camera.

Within a day or so I had slipped back into the smooth wilderness routines; but it soon became starkly and frustratingly clear that the week at Phantom had forced me partway back into the rhythms and thoughtways of civilization. Five days passed before I succeeded in returning my mind to the Canyon.

For two days I hurried eastward along the Tonto Trail, photographing copiously, seeing only the surface of things. The third day I took a short-cut trail up and over the Redwall. On top, on Horseshoe Mesa, I found the ruins of an old mining camp. For two hours I wandered among its handful of tottering and tottered buildings. I examined rusty machinery. I handled trenchant relics: fragments of blue glass, a chipped dish, a battered kerosene lamp. I looked long and thoughtfully at many warped and weathered timbers and listened to them creaking in the wind. But the place, barely sixty years dead, refused to crackle into life. I heard no echoes, met no wraiths gliding across the worn wooden thresholds.

On the fourth morning a crack at last opened in the flat surface of the present. I had camped in a dry watercourse that ran down the center of a sidecanyon. I woke in half-light and lay looking up and off to my left at a vertical bank, eight or ten feet high, that a flash flood had scoured out of the canyon floor. And as I lay watching daylight fill in the details of the boulders and stones and sand that made up this bank, the flood that had created the bank was suddenly so real that I could almost see the last few grains of sand dribbling down into its receding waters. And for a few minutes then, as I lay half awake, more than the creation of the bank was real. I could feel and understand and accept and believe in, utterly, the whole long and continuous process that had stripped rock fragments from the cliffs above and then had dropped them, boulder by stone by grain of sand, until at last they accumulated into the gravelly soil that now covered the floor of the sidecanyon. For those few minutes, the slow building-up of the talus and then the sudden scouring-away that had created the bank stood out as vividly and surely as the story of the rocks had done on the day I walked down Bass Trail. The time scales of this bank and this talus were pitifully short, of course; I knew that. And my understanding soon faded. But the important thing was that it had happened. That there had been a break, a promise.

On the evening of the fifth day the promise was at last fulfilled.

There were, I am sure, many contributory reasons. Our moods, like our motives, are rarely simple. By now I had mastered all but one of the week's physical challenges. And I had undermined the hegemony of my new camera. Above all, I had walked for five days in silence and solitude. And day after sunlit day the silence and the solitude had been caressing me, easing me back almost physically toward the serene world I had walked through during those long, rhythmic days along the Tonto Platform before I went down to Phantom. On the evening of the fifth day an unexpected burst of excitement brought me once more to the brink of that world. And what finally nudged me back was an unexpected meeting.

The night before, I had camped at Hance Rapids. These rapids mark the point at which the Tonto Platform finally tapers away. (They also mark the eastern limit of the wild-burro territory. The burros' eastward spread seems to have been blocked either by the rough country ahead or by a radical change in the vegetation on which they depend for food.) The only route that Harvey Butchart knew of beyond the Platform involved at least two days of scrambling along narrow, tortuously folded terraces, a thousand feet and more above the river. But the river, running lower than it ever had before, now offered a possible alternative. With luck I might just be able to make my way along close beside it. Although Harvey had seemed doubtful about such a route, I decided to give it a try. But I knew that if I failed and then had to tackle the terraces afterward, my schedule for meeting the airdrop would be squeezed desperately tight.

When, early on the fifth morning beyond Phantom, I left the Hance Rapids nightcamp, my hopes for the river route stood high. The hard, dark rock of the Gorge had almost vanished, dipping down and away to the east. Ahead, a soft red shale promised easier going. By the time I had walked upriver for an hour the steep black rock had finally slanted away underground; and, just as I had hoped, the red shale talus sloped at a comparatively gentle angle. My hopes gained altitude.

The hopes soared, I think, on more than severely practical breezes. Above Hance Rapids the Gorge was no longer a gloomy place, even objectively. Talus and cliff rose red and cheerful. The river swirled blue-green and sparkling. At the mouth of each sidecanyon it had long ago padded the bare rock with sand. Now bright green bushes and even a few optimistic willow trees helped soften the scene.

All morning I made steady progress through this genial landscape. Twice, impassable rock buttresses that thrust out into the river forced me to make air-mattress detours. In the ninety-degree morning heat a swim should have been an enticing prospect; but I still stood and fought something of my old battle before I slid into the water and dog-paddled up a hundred feet of slow-moving current with the carefully waterproofed pack half floating, half supported over one shoulder. Afterward I felt only a hint of elation: the skirmish had been too tame for any great reward. But even this mild spur did its bit to help the day forward. (The detours were valuable practice too. I knew that somewhere up ahead I would have to swim across the Colorado: the final airdrop site and my exit route both lay on the far side of the river.)

By late afternoon I could see a long, curving cliff, four or five hundred feet high, rising sheer and red from the river. It was, I knew, the last obstacle before my airdrop site. The map had suggested that I might be able to by-pass the cliff up a sidecanyon; now I saw through binoculars that there was also a chance I might be able to find a route along its foot, past white and roaring rapids.

It turned out to be an exciting place, the foot of that cliff. I picked my way forward along rock slabs that angled up and out from the foot of the cliff and then sliced off sheer into the river. To the left, sometimes only inches below my boots, the water raced past in steep, muttering waves. To my right, the slabs often slanted down and away into blue, crystal-clear pools that the receding river had left between tilted slab and sheer cliff face. At times, the strip of rock protruding above water level narrowed to plank-width. Slowly and carefully I moved upstream along these slabs toward the heart of the rapids. The surging waves mounted closer to my boots; grew whiter, faster, louder. The slabs narrowed.

And all the time the cliff was almost overwhelming me with its bulk and beauty and threat. Its bulk, because there was nothing else beyond my right shoulder: just the unbearable weight of solid rock. Its beauty, because time and the river had sculptured the whole cliff face into snaggle-toothed projections, each shape sharp and angular, each surface smooth, each pattern a dazzle-contrast of deep rich red and, where a projection blocked the setting sun, almost impenetrable black. Its threat most of all: because every shelving projection seemed to hang poised directly above my head; because on every shelf rested precarious fragments of rock that had paused there on an inevitable downward path; and, most vividly of all, because I had to pick my way forward through rubble that had presumably fallen from the cliff face in the half-stutter of geologic time since the last Colorado flood swept like a liquid broom across the submerged slabs. Some of the fallen rocks looked big enough to wreck a house. Not one of them, it seemed to me, was small enough to land after a fall of even fifty feet without crushing a man's skull to pulp.

There was something else, too, about those slanting red slabs: I knew I was the first man to walk along them. Now, a wild place will often lure you into such a titillating thought; but usually, when you force yourself to be honest, you know you are probably wrong. This time I was as sure as a man can ever be: the slabs hardly protruded above water; the closing of Glen Canyon Dam had dropped the river to this, its record low level, only two months earlier; and according to Park Headquarters no one had been down into this section of the Canyon since that time. I found myself moving forward along the slabs, picking my way through the fallen red rubble, with a mounting and quite unexpected sense of excitement.*

The crisis came near the far end of the cliff. From a distance I had not been able to see, even through binoculars, whether the slabs finally vanished altogether just below the heart of the rapids or merely tapered to a narrow shelf before broadening out again into a clearly visible platform. As I approached the critical point, in the last of the day's sunlight, the uncertainty remained. The slabs kept tapering away into the cliff face, but always there was another for me to transfer to. I traversed the last few yards along a miniature reef, sharply tilted. The waves surged very close now, steeper, taller, even louder. Ten paces to go, and

---

*Long after I left the Canyon I discovered that I was, after all, not quite right about the river's low level. The day I passed under the cliff, the Colorado's flow near Phantom Ranch was 1,260 cubic feet per second. In the forty years during which accurate records have been kept, the flow has dropped below this figure for a short time on one occasion (Dec. 28, 1924: 990 cubic feet per second). But it remains highly improbable, to say the least, that anyone had ever been along under the face of that remote cliff.

still uncertainty. And then I saw, two feet above the water, jutting out from the smooth cliff face, a four-inch-wide ledge. It turned six feet of impossibility into a cakewalk. A few moments of surprisingly easy edging forward and I stood on the far side, at the beginning of a broad platform. Soon water no longer raced below my feet, rock no longer overhung my head. The way to the airdrop lay open.

I walked on upriver. The sun had set now, and after the roar of white water the evening was very quiet. I walked slowly, looking for a campsite. I wanted a good camp this time, not just somewhere to sleep: it was barely a mile to the airdrop site, and with the last barrier past I had two full days to spare.

I clambered around a rocky spur and walked out onto a sand bar. A thicket of bushes choked its center, but along the edge, on top of a six-foot bank that curved around a backwater of the river, ran a narrow strip of sand. As I moved out onto this strip the day began to ease across that mysterious, half-world threshold that leads over into night. And it was then that I saw them.

It must have been movement that caught my attention, for they were as silent as the sand and the thicket. At first I saw only two small shapes moving slowly along the backwater, close under the bank. Then there were four of them. Four flat, dark heads, half-submerged. Four neat uptilted noses cutting unhurried V's across the surface of the water. I stood and watched, motionless. The noses went on circling. Once a broad tail lifted and slapped down and a curved body arched up and over. For a while there were only three heads, three noses. Then the fourth reappeared, cutting its deliberate V across the quiet, darkening backwater.

Soon one of the heads stopped at the foot of the

bank, directly below my feet. I could see, quite clearly, its sleek, furry texture. Could see, embedded in the fur, catching the last of the light, a single bright eye. The eye looked up at me. Looked and looked, unblinking. Then, apparently satisfied that I posed no threat, eye and animal resumed their cruise.

I must have stood on the bank for fifteen or twenty minutes looking down at these, the first beavers I had ever seen. Perhaps I stood there much longer, held by the warm sense of privilege you get from watching truly wild animals at close quarters—the feeling that you have been let in on a momentous secret. But at last, knowing I ought to make camp before dark, I moved quietly forward.

Six paces, and I stopped. From a little bundle of sticks on the bank, twenty feet ahead, came a familiar buzzing. Slowly, so as not to disturb the beavers, I made unthreatening passes with my staff. The snake was pale pink, about three feet long, and as pathetically frightened as most disturbed rattlesnakes are. After a minute or two it slid sideways into the thicket. When I walked on I gave a respectfully wide berth to the place it had disappeared. But our meeting had been a quiet and gentlemanly affair. It had in no way disturbed the evening's new warmth and harmony.

Almost at once I came to the tangle of neatly bitten-off sticks that was the beavers' lodge. Prodding ahead with my staff (I was undeniably more aware of rattlesnakes now, the way you always are after meeting one) I bypassed the lodge through the thicket. Beyond, the sand bar swung out to a point. When I reached the point I stopped and looked back.

The light had almost gone, but I could just see that two of the beavers had come up out of the water and were browsing along a shelf at the foot of the sandy bank. On land they looked ungainly, humpbacked creatures. They moved slowly and awkwardly, along the very edge of the lapping backwater. Every few steps they paused to pluck straggles of vegetation and lift them to their mouths with surprising deftness in forepaws held piously together.

I stood watching the silent and strangely solemn scene. There was something almost too primordial about it, I decided—as if the beavers had moved back into a time before their own. For it seemed to me, though I was not sure why, the sort of scene you would have expected to find if you had stood on the margin of a marsh in the hot and humid heyday of the dinosaurs.

I camped close to the point, under a willow tree that grew on the edge of a small clearing, thirty yards from the beaver lodge. I did not light a fire, and I prepared dinner very quietly: the beavers seemed to have accepted my presence, the way wild animals sometimes will if you approach quietly enough and at a lucky moment, but I wanted to take no chances. Flickering flames or heavy footsteps or the metallic rattle of spoon against cooking pot might send the whole family diving for the submerged entrance to their lodge. When I lit my noisy pressure stove I found myself imagining, all too vividly, that down inside the lodge's tangle of sticks four pairs of pained beaver eyes had lifted to Beaver Heaven and a quartet of sleek, damp voices was muttering: "Oh, Beaver Christ!"

But all through dinner I kept hearing the occasional slap of a broad tail on water. And soon after I stretched out for the night on my air mattress and pulled the unzipped sleeping bag over my naked body (for several nights now it had been too hot to sleep inside the bag), one of the beavers cruised out of the backwater, passed my camp, and patrolled away upriver. I had no trouble tracing its progress: every few moments, at irregular intervals, its tail slapped explosively down. I found myself listening to the sounds, trying for some reason to define them, or at least to fit them into the elusive jigsaw of experience. It seemed likely to be an unprofitable exercise: after all, these were the first beavers I had ever met. But I kept on listening. Listening intently. Each explosion was a heavy, distinctive "Ker-PLOOOOOSH," as if two boulders had been heaved into the water almost simultaneously. There was, I felt, something strangely familiar about the sound. And all at once, quite unexpectedly, lying there on the sand bar looking up at pale stars in a moonlit sky and listening intently to the patrolling beaver, I heard the answer to a long-standing question that I thought had long ago been answered.

Five years before, during a summer-long, thousand-mile walk through the deserts and mountains of California, I had camped just like this beside the Colorado, three hundred miles downstream of the Canyon. That night too had been star-filled and flooded with moonlight. And as I lay on the threshold of sleep I had heard, exactly like this, an irregular succession of splashes out in the darkness of a back eddy. The splashes had passed close to my camp, circled the eddy several times, then swung out into the main river and tapered away, fainter and fainter, until at last I could once more hear only the river talking to the night. That camp, I had known, would be my last beside the Colorado before I swung westward across the Mojave Desert; and in the sounds of the splashes I had heard, though I was not sure why, the hint of a secret I shared with the Colorado. And hints of deeper secrets too.

I had remembered that night, remembered it vividly. And later I had tried to write it down in a book. In both memory and book I assumed that the splashes had come from a jumping fish. While I lay listening to them my mind had harbored doubts: the sound was almost right, but not quite. Afterward, because "jumping fish" seemed the only explanation, my doubts had faded, the way they tend to in such cases.

But now, in a single flash of memory, the doubts were confirmed—and resolved. I knew, as certainly as if I had been able to peer back five years through blue desert darkness and watch a broad tail slap down on swirling water, that the sounds had not after all come from a jumping fish. For this time, here in the Canyon, the sound was right. Dead right.

And all at once I saw that the discovery made a perfect end to the day. For I had already sensed, without quite knowing it, that on this starry and moonlit night too the Colorado had told me, or was preparing to tell me, some new and valuable secret.

I camped for two days on Beaver Sand Bar. Two restful and receptive days. I did not do very much, really. Nothing at all that was even mildly dramatic. But every minute of the days held meaning.

It was on the first morning, I think, that I realized I was no longer very interested in the sheer physical magnificence of the Canyon. High above me towered the Palisades of the Desert: mile after mile of colossal, echeloned, exquisitely colored cliffs that rose almost sheer for more than three thousand feet. A year before, in my first moment of shock on the Rim, it was the Palisades that had, more than any other sight, overwhelmed me. Yet now, I realized, they no longer impressed me. I had come to accept towering magnificence as the natural state of the world. And when the days were right I was looking behind the magnificence for the meanings.

My journey, in other words, had once again moved on. During the rhythmic days between Bass and Phantom I had felt, with a new sense of inclusion, that I was an integral part of a web-in-time: rock and agave and bee, lizard and rattlesnake and wild burro, Indian and Welshman. But now, on Beaver Sand Bar, came a sense not only of inclusion but of affinity.

The sand bar did not quite recapture for me, oddly enough, the solemn rhythms of geologic time. But I heard with sharper clarity, as if I had moved closer to the source, that variation on "the unique basic rhythm" which seems to have sprung spontaneously from the measured rhythm of the rocks: the variation that has surged forward with ever-increasing strength and complexity. I had moved back inside my natural museum. And this time I found myself in a gallery marked "History of Life."

Afterward, I found it difficult to say just when the break came. Perhaps it was when I looked back and saw the two beavers browsing along the margin of the backwater, silent and solemn and almost unnaturally primordial. Or perhaps it was when the patrolling beaver solved the unasked riddle of the jumping fish. All I knew for sure was that very soon, in that peaceful place, I seemed to have moved back into a time before my own, just as the beavers had seemed to me to have moved back into the age of the dinosaurs. Now I had moved back and down into an age before the coming of man, the noisy animal. It was almost a physical thing, that descent; as physical as the descent of Bass Trail had been, back and down into the history of the rocks.

The present did not surrender Beaver Sand Bar

quite without resistance. During the two days I lived there I stumbled on several undeniable anachronisms that the river had swept down into that ancient world: a log sawn straight at one end; a splintered railroad tie; a black distributor cap wedged between two rocks; and, of all things, a child's toy—a plastic jet fighter plane, pale blue. I do not think I made any particular effort to thrust such reminders away; I just stood and looked at them and smiled and did not, I am sure, quite believe.

The sand bar, I discovered, was alive. It did not seethe with obvious life, the way a meadow can. The Canyon is never like that. But in the due course of time I met, inmate by diffident inmate, a remarkably full house.

The beavers continued to leave the broadest imprint on the days. Early the first morning I went down to the river to refill my canteens. And fifteen paces from my willow tree, on smooth sand, I found the tracks of an animal that had pulled itself up, dripping wet, onto the bank. It had climbed, I saw, just high enough for a clear view of the orange-shrouded shape that lay at the foot of the willow tree; and then it had slithered back down into the river, leaving a six-inch-wide mark in eloquent testimony of a tail dragged rather carelessly along behind.

I must have passed this second test for harmlessness too, for all that afternoon I watched and photographed a lone beaver loafing the sunlit hours away. At first I crouched behind a bush at a safe hundred-yard range. The animal ignored me. Slowly I moved closer. In the end I was sitting out on an open bank, barely a dozen paces away from it.

Mostly the beaver rested, awash, on the submerged point of a sandspit. Sometimes it patrolled the river, swimming slowly, head uptilted, so that all I could see from a distance was a shiny black nose at the tip of a fuzzy brown face. (Fuzzy and no longer sleek, and brown, not black, because sun and wind soon dried out the fur.) When it passed close I could see, under water, its whole slim and streamlined body. Stretched out like that from tip of nose to tip of tail, it seemed to measure between four and five feet. Two or three times the beaver made landfall on a midstream island. It climbed ashore and sat up on its haunches, looking surprisingly bulky, and examined some tidbit held between extended forepaws. But it always came back to its favorite sandspit. Each time, it grounded gently on the point. And there, barely a dozen paces away from me, it squatted. Awash. Wet and black and shining. Humpbacked. Statuesque. Imperturbable.

I was stupidly surprised to find that in profile the beaver had the pointed face and underslung mouth of a typical rodent. Yet it looked not so much like a huge mouse (for a mouse is a tremulous, flexible, squeeze-through-anything kind of creature) as like a blown-up version of one of those toy rubber mice that manage to look as unrealistically solid as bulldogs. I do not mean, of course, that this beaver looked at all like a bulldog. It was far too sleek and streamlined. But squatting there half submerged, with ripples lapping lazily against its wet fur, it had the solid and self-assured air you would expect in, say, a Victorian haberdasher. A man who throughout an exemplary life had haberdashed conscientiously and eaten well and exercised sparingly and now, in the sunlit afternoon of his days, liked to leave serious business to his wife and children and other underlings while he sat and meditated in his favorite chair, wrapped against the outside possibility of a chill in the sleek beaver coat that was his symbol of success. My beaver, in other words, sat at ease on its favorite sandbank, relaxed

and confident, with none of the fear-triggered alert-
ness that is the necessary life-frame of most wild
animals. Beavers have few natural enemies; almost
the only serious one is man. And it was abundantly
clear that for the placid beaver I sat watching down
in my quiet sand-bar-world of the past, man did not
yet exist.

Most of that long, hot afternoon I watched the
beaver through binoculars. At times, the sleek black
shape almost filled their field. Now, when you look
through binoculars you see through a glass, brightly:
magnification and stereoscopic effect give your vision
an extra dimension of vividness. And hour after hour
that afternoon I seemed to float just above the water,
so close to the resting beaver that I felt I ought to be
breathing quietly in order to avoid disturbing it. In
the end I felt as if I had in some very real way moved
inside its rodent world. I felt that I knew exactly what
it was like to squat on a sandspit out in a wide, wave-
crinkled river and loaf away a summer afternoon.
What it was like to swim luxuriously, because of some
uncomprehended urge, in long, easy arcs, upriver and
down, with my eyes barely above the wave crests. To
make landfall occasionally and come waddling up out
of the water into hot sunshine so that I could lift some
newfound treasure in my forepaws and examine it. To
be vaguely conscious, all the time, that out on the
bank sat a large, pinkish, mildly hairy newcomer to
my world—a strange creature I would perhaps not
altogether trust, but which I had twice checked out
as harmless.

The beavers, of course, were only the beginning of
Beaver Sand Bar.

After dinner that second evening, as I lay in the
darkness under my willow tree thinking late-evening
thoughts or nonthoughts, I heard a faint, Lilliputian

rustle. I switched on my flashlight, and there, less than two feet from my eyes, sat a tiny mouse. Its dark brown body—shading to white on all four legs and on the underside of the tail—was smooth and strokable, and its big, intelligent-looking eyes stared directly into mine. I say that this mouse "sat." But it is quite the wrong word, really. It gives far too static a picture of a creature that was, every second, the whiskered epitome of quivering nervousness. A creature filled with the incessant, fluttering, wild-animal-fear mobility that had been so notably absent from the placid beaver squatting monumentally on its sandspit.

For half an hour I lay and watched the mouse.* It was a fascinating little creature, quick and clean and lively. Mostly it scurried about the sand, scraping the surface and chewing feverishly at whatever tidbits it turned up. But from time to time it would race off on sudden and quite unpredictable forays up slender willow stems. Once it nibbled speculatively at a red plastic canteen stopper I had filled with sugar-flavored water and had taped to a willow stem to attract hummingbirds. But, so far as I could see, it gained nothing from these sudden excursions.

Every movement the mouse made was thistledown delicate. When it scurried around the lip of my cooking-pot lid, which lay precariously balanced on a small log, the lid did not even tilt. On its willow-wand forays, the slender stems it raced along barely began to bend. And after a while, as I lay and watched the tremulous brown body and racing white legs, I found myself beginning to know what it must be like to scrape and nose among coarse grains of sand; to live,

---

*It was almost certainly a deer mouse (academically, *Peromyscus maniculatus:* "pouched mouse with small hands"). Deer mice are not at all well-known to the general public. And this is odd, because next to *Homo sapiens* they are the most widely distributed species of native mammal in the United States.

always, so close to starvation that from habit you attack every morsel of food with feverish anxiety; to
dash unexpectedly and for reasons you do not in the
least understand up broad willow stems. Above all I
felt something of the joy there must be in making
every movement with the delicacy of thistledown. As
a mouse, you would probably not feel joy in the conscious way we humans do; but as I watched this agile
little creature I felt the joy as clearly as when I
watched a seven-foot-one-inch athlete, the greatest
basketball player in the world, reach up and over
three straining opponents and fingertip the ball into
the hoop before he pirouetted out and away with the
grace and delicacy of a ballerina, his sweating face
eased for a moment into a massive, gentle smile of
satisfaction, a smile that revealed, quite unconsciously, the sheer joy of perfected achievement. Lying there on the sand under my willow tree, peering
along the beam of my flashlight, I felt the common
fiber that ran through the tiptoe delicacy of both gigantic man and tiny mouse; and I understood, im-
probably, their single strand of joy.

There was one thing about the mouse that I must
admit I quite failed to understand: it hardly seemed
to notice my flashlight beam. Sometimes, when I
switched the light on, it paused. Once or twice it
peered quizzically up the beam. But most often it ignored the light completely. And this is something I
have never been able to comprehend, whether the animal is cat, ant bear, or mouse. Whatever the cool,
optical explanation, I cannot put myself wholly in the
place of an animal that betrays almost no recognition
of the change from pitch blackness to dazzling flood-
light.

But while I lived on Beaver Sand Bar I found that,
by and large, I understood the other animals. Some-

times I even understood without meeting them. When I followed a spoor that skirted the water's edge from one end of the sand bar to the other, print after regular print, I grasped something of how it must feel to wander, as coyotes do, thirty or forty miles in a night. When I found a massive paw mark, three and a half inches across, I knew the fringes of being an outsize bobcat or a smallish mountain lion padding silently over soft sand.

But all these animals—beaver and mouse, coyote and lion—were mammals; and, even when we are buried deep in civilization, nothing but very flimsy barriers separates us from the other twigs on our own branch of life. It is only when we move back down the trunk of genealogy to creatures whose stock long ago split off from ours that a sense of affinity becomes difficult. When your dog wags his tail, you understand his pleasure; but how does a slug indicate that it is pleased? And do you honestly feel that you could comprehend its pleasure? But on Beaver Sand Bar, though I did not quite realize it at the time, I began to move, step by step, back and down our genealogical tree.

I shared my clearing with several resident lizards: a corpulent, yellow-masked character that faced obvious psychological problems when a quiet promenade along a log brought it face to face with my pink toothbrush; an individual with a sharply pointed nose who happened to be passing by when I stood urinating on the sand and who swerved off course to take a bonus shower with every sign of enjoyment; and an orange-cap with dragon-rough scales and spiky gill-frills who slipped off a branch of the willow tree and plopped so unexpectedly onto the sand two inches from my elbow as I lay jotting down some notes that I am not sure which of us was the more startled.

Now, a lizard, although a reptile, makes easy hu-

man understanding. It is an alert, quick-reacting creature, not at all obviously cold-blooded. Although its
skin is very different from ours, it has four limbs. And
its eyelids make its eyes look passably like what is a
human's most expressive feature. These chance details are important. They make it easy for us to let
our minds move, quite unconsciously, of course, "inside" another animal. Even in your back garden, a
lizard basking on a stone is likely to furnish you with
glimmerings of what it feels like to bask, slim and
scaly, on a warm, rough stone.

A snake is also a reptile. Genealogically speaking,
it is the lizard's next-door neighbor. But, humanly
speaking, a gulf separates them. A snake has no legs,
no eyelids. And we are conditioned to regard it as the
epitome of evil. So most of us do not, I think, normally find our minds moving "inside" a snake's body.

But on Beaver Sand Bar it was a rattlesnake that
carried me back and down over the first serious barrier to understanding. I am almost sure it was the
same gentlemanly rattlesnake that had greeted me the
first evening. It was the same pale shade of pink and
roughly the same three-foot length. And we met in almost exactly the same place. (Rattlers rarely move far;
some seem to live out their entire lives within a ra-
dius of a hundred feet or so.)

Now, I am no rattlesnake *aficionado*. The first rattler I met scared me purple, and killing it seemed a
human duty. That meeting took place beside the Colorado too, near the start of the same thousand-mile
walk on which I heard the "jumping fish." Yet by the
end of that California summer I no longer felt an un-
reasoning fear of rattlers. Unless they lived danger-
ously close to places frequented by people, and
especially by children, I no longer killed them. Instead, I accepted them as organisms with a niche in

the web of life. Accepted them, that is, as fellow creatures. I do not think I felt the coupling very deeply, but at least I had overcome the most numbing effects of fear. Later I grew interested enough in rattlesnakes to write a magazine article about them. In researching it I assimilated the entire two volumes and 1,500-odd pages of the subject's last-word technical bible. By then I knew a lot of facts about rattlesnakes. But I remained an observer, rigidly outside their world. And I remained sharply aware that they are dangerous creatures. The less often our paths crossed in the wild, the happier I would be.

Grand Canyon rattlesnakes, that subspecies so neatly named *abyssus*, have a reputation for being an amiable crowd by rattlesnake standards, and my three meetings with them so far had certainly seemed to generate no real malice or threat on either side. Perhaps that is why, when I glanced back into the thicket as I sat on the bank of Beaver Sand Bar and saw a pale-pink rattlesnake come gliding over the sand, barely six feet away from me, I felt curiosity rather than fear. The snake was clearly unaware of my presence. Slowly, gracefully, it threaded its way through a forest of willow shoots. As its flank pushed past each stem I could see the individual scales tilt under the stem's pressure, then move back flush. Four feet from my left buttock the snake stopped, its head in a sun-dappled patch of sand beside a cluster of roots. Unhurriedly, it drew its body forward and curled into a flat resting coil. Then it stretched and yawned. It yawned a long and unmistakable yawn. A yawn so uninhibited that for many slow seconds I seemed to see nothing but the pale lining of its mouth and two matching arcs of small, sharp teeth. When the yawn was over at last, the snake raised its head and twisted it slowly and luxuriously from side to side, as a man or woman will do in anticipation of rest and comfort to come. Finally, with such obvious contentment that I do not think I would have been very surprised to hear the creature purr, it laid its head gently on the pillow of its clean and beautifully marked body.

And all at once, for the first time in my life, I found I had moved "inside" a rattlesnake. Quite unexpectedly, I had shared its sleepiness and anticipation and contentment. And as I sat looking down at the sleeping snake coiled in its patch of sun-dappled shade, I found myself feeling for it something remarkably close to affection.*

On the second morning I woke under the willow tree to find myself looking, at a range of barely a foot, full into the slit-eyes of a toad that sat enthroned on my sugar box. I sat up. The toad, sensing danger, jumped accurately into a cooking pot. But just before it jumped I understood, for a brief instant, the alarm that had surged through it. Carefully, I lifted the toad out of the water that half filled the pot. I would like to say that I felt both its astonishment at being confined in a smooth metal prison and also its relief at escape. But I detected neither. Perhaps a toad is too far back for such emotions. Or, rather, is too far back

---

*When this book was almost ready for publication, I read with astonishment and dismay in Konrad Lorenz's fascinating book, *On Aggression*, the statement that "birds and reptiles lack the motor pattern of yawning."

I immediately wrote to Dr. Lorenz. He replied: "The question of yawning arises with many readers of my book, because I did not state clearly enough that by yawning, as defined by Heinroth, 1910, I mean a motor coordination in which the dorsal muscles of the neck and partly also of the back are contracted, the mouth is opened to the utmost extent, while simultaneously the chest is expanded in maximum inspiration. Reptiles and birds may occasionally stretch their jaw muscles, maximally opening their mouths, but among them there is no coordination with any breathing movements."

That left me perfectly happy. I am quite free to say that what I saw was no doubt a rudimentary activity from which the full yawning process of mammals eventually evolved. Having watched that rattlesnake act, to all appearances, in exactly the way a sleepy human might act under similar circumstances, I harbor no doubts at all about my contention. But I don't, thank God, have to prove anything.

for us to recognize in it the rudiments from which sprang these emotions we now feel so unmistakably.

With the toad, of course, I had barely begun to move back down our family tree. Toads are amphibians, the reptiles' predecessors. They are the remnants of those "failures of the sea" who first colonized the land. Those failures who expended their vitality (without, of course, any inkling of what they were about) in opening up a new world and keeping it spinning for a while until individuals better adjusted to the new conditions moved in and did the dull but necessary job of organizing things. (In this case, the better-adjusted individuals were those who by chance mutation turned out to be more efficient at such newly necessary acts as breathing air and propelling their bodies without the support of water: the reptiles.)

The amphibians' immediate predecessors were fish. I caught several catfish on Beaver Sand Bar. Yet rather surprisingly—for I grew up so addicted to trout fishing that I spent half my young life trying to think like a trout—I do not remember that I even began to move "inside" any of the catfish. But then, unlike the other animals, the catfish were food. The moment I lifted one of them out of the river with my walking-staff-and-nylon tackle I put it out of pain by breaking its neck. And I no doubt shielded myself from pain by shutting my mind to all hint of affinity.

Now, fish too lie only a short way back down our family tree. But beyond them yawns a gap that we humans find hard to bridge. For fish were the first organisms to generate an apparatus that they have handed down, basically unchanged, to all amphibians and reptiles and birds and mammals. They "invented" the backbone. This astonishingly successful device holds us together in a more than physical and individual sense: it makes us a kind of club. And, as often happens to members of exclusive clubs, we tend to run into difficulties of understanding when we look outside. In this case we look out at the backboneless creatures, or invertebrates.

I can remember, just once, in a moment of purest euphoria, feeling glad for a cloud of mosquitoes that they were alive. Glad for their sakes, I mean. (This moment also occurred during that long summer's walk up California; I begin to see that during those earlier months of space and silence and solitude I learned the rudiments of many things the Canyon later taught me more explicitly. But then, I suppose it would be surprising if that were not the case.) The bridge across which I made some kind of contact with those California mosquitoes was a flimsy and short-lived affair. On Beaver Sand Bar I twice found myself trying to cross, through insects, the gap that separates us from the invertebrates.

The first attempt ended in total failure. Out of the night and into my flashlight beam zoomed a large brown insect that I immediately thought of as a dragonfly, though I knew I was technically wrong. The three-inch-long creature settled on a stone, facing head-on into a wind that kept gusting across the sand bar. During each gust it folded its wings tight and gripped the stone with its six long legs. I reached into a pocket of my pack and found my ten-power prospector's magnifying glass. As I moved in on the dragonfly (you have to get really close with such lenses, almost touching) it showed signs of unrest. I huffed and puffed, downwind. The dragonfly folded its wings tighter and gripped the stone even more firmly. I peered through the magnifying glass—into an astonishing gnat's-eye-view peepshow, brilliantly floodlit by my flashlight beam. Through the tiny lens I could bring into focus at any one time only a small portion of the now-gigantic animal. First, shining brown body plates: massive, iridescent, impenetrable. Then huge, barbed-wire-hairy legs. Then the waving antennae, thick and solid, constructed of ring joined to ring joined to ring, like a worm. Then a bulbous, astonishing eye: a surface of many curving lenses, close-fitting, like a multi-faceted jewel but far more cunningly fashioned; behind this surface, a cavernous structure of angled prisms, some reflecting a brilliant blue light, some admitting the light to new, many-angled, blue-mirrored galleries; the whole eye more like an impossibly perfect man-made apparatus than any "natural" phenomenon, but beautiful, and, at the same time, because of the unexpectedness, appalling. Finally, horribly, the face: a pulsating maze of hairy pincers and dark, devouring space. That space, I knew, must have been the final terrifying prospect seen by many a doomed gnat.

But I thought this thought with only the superficial, intellectual sector of my mind. Try as I might, I remained divorced from the bizarre reality beyond the lens; it was too remote in its reference points from anything I had ever experienced. For ten minutes I peered through the lens, utterly fascinated. But I failed to move even part way out across the gap dividing me from the world it revealed. I could not, without proper preparation, wrest myself free from the outside world of the sand bar. At the time I felt a sense of failure. But afterward I saw that crossing the gap that evening would have been almost as difficult as trying to move directly and without preparation from the man-centered world of civilization—in which we also tend to see everything from firmly within the confines of our time and size and position—into the world of the Canyon's museum.

Next afternoon I did rather better. I was lying sprawled out on the hot sand, naked. I was doing, as far as I remember, nothing. Now, interludes in which you sprawl and do nothing are great occasions for seeing important things that you have always been too busy to notice. And after I had lain there for a long time, with my eyes just above the glaring and granular sand, I noticed a fly. A fly so small that even to my ground-level eyes it had little more than existence. It was, I mean, just a dark speck with no particular shape or character. This fly—which I cleverly classified as a sandfly, though I had no idea what it was—kept recrystallizing into my field of vision. And always, when I saw it, it was moving along the same zigzag and vaguely pugnacious route. Before long I had mapped out its routine.

From its resting position on the sand it would for no reason immediately apparent to me soar into the air at an oblique angle. It flew straight—straight as a foot rule, and just about as far. And then, without warning, its path intersected that of another sandfly. The paths fused. Fused into a spherical blur. A blur so blurred that I had no idea whether the two tiny bodies, presumably gyrating in orbit, ever made contact. Almost at once the blur resolved: one sandfly streaked away out of my field of vision; the other swooped down into a zigzag, pugnacious patrol, an inch above the sand. This patrol took it, four or five times in three or four seconds, around the imaginary perimeter of a patch of sand about a foot wide and two feet long. Its patrol completed, the sandfly settled in the place from which it had taken off.

Every few minutes the drama was rerun, inches

from my eyes: rest, interception; dogfight; patrol; rest. Of course I had no means of proving that it was always the original sandfly that emerged from the dogfight to patrol and rest and fight again, but after five or six performances there was no longer room for reasonable doubt: the patrol always circled the same imaginary perimeter, and the fly always came back to rest on exactly the same little hillock of sand. It seemed abundantly clear that this tiny sandfly had its own jealously guarded territory.

I should not have been surprised, I suppose. Many animals behave this way. Certain birds and mammals in particular. They stand on constant pugnacious guard against any incursion into what they consider their rightful territories: their own corner of a wood, their patch of scrub, their lawn, their nation, their natural continental sphere of influence. The patch of sand my sandfly guarded had no visible boundaries; but the patrols traced its outline so regularly that before long I could almost see the territory mapped out on the glaring, uneven sand as an elongated lozenge of an island. At times it looked rather like Cuba. At others, suspiciously like Formosa.

Perhaps it was this loaded geography lesson that built the bridge. Anyway, I know that before long I found that I had, mentally speaking, picked my cumbersome self up off the sand and moved "inside" that tiny speck of a sandfly. When it took off on one of its interception missions I felt something of its injured pride and something of the helpless, automatic anger that projected it, willy-nilly, into the blur that was presumably a dogfight. I felt, in other words, the fly-equivalent of clenched fists—the equivalent of rattling sabers, of waiting ICBM's. And lying there with my eyes close to the glaring and granular sand with the clearly imprinted but invisible island and its pugnacious and barely visible defender, I saw human war as something quite luminously explicable. Explicable, but not a buzz or a bluff less stupid.*

And after that I no longer seemed to need examples. I no longer needed to concentrate on a deer mouse or a rattlesnake or a sandfly. For I was no longer a stranger in the deep and ancient world of Beaver Sand Bar. And I could move about almost freely, it seemed, through those long, quiet corridors of time that angle up and away from the first simple fragments of animate life.

I do not mean that I gained any new intellectual insight. My animal meetings had taught me no important new facts. Nothing at all that would help me to understand more clearly, in any intellectual sense, how all the scattered and disparate strands of life weave together, interlocking. But I had moved closer to the pulse of life. I had heard a new counterpoint to the unique basic rhythm of the universe. And in it I recognized the common grain that ran through everything I knew existed, including me.

We all of us experience this oceanic feeling, I think, at some time or other. Its surge had been there, strong but still far off, at the end of my thousand-mile California walk. Now, on Beaver Sand Bar, the sense of union had become explicit, intimate, totally involving. It embraced everything. Not only man and beaver and mouse, lizard and rattlesnake and toad, sandfly and slug. Not only thicket and willow tree. Not only the sand bar. But the rock as well. The rock from which the sand bar's sand had been fashioned. The rock that was the foundation across which and probably from

---

*At that time, Robert Ardrey's *Territorial Imperative* (1966) had not been published. Anyone who would like to investigate the potentially species-fatal phenomenon of human war as a natural process of animal evolution could hardly do better than read this book. It is both entertaining and thought-provoking.

which had been stretched the whole pulsating, interlocking web of life. And with the rock and the plants
and the animals, even with the wind and its cloud
shadows, I felt, now, a sense of common origin and
direction. A sense of union so vibrant that when I
looked back afterward I sometimes felt that the whole
experience on Beaver Sand Bar was like a perfect act
of physical love. For the union was total and natural
and selfish and unselfish and beautiful and holy, and
at the same time riotously good fun. And while it
lasted nothing else mattered, nothing else existed.

MAN

—

ON THE morning of the eighth day beyond Phantom I moved a mile upriver to the airdrop site.

By that time I knew, more clearly than I had at any other stage of my journey, exactly what I would be looking for next. I would take the logical step forward from Beaver Sand Bar. I would spend my final two weeks in the Canyon finding out what its museum had to tell me about that astonishingly successful newcomer, the animal that dominates today's world. The museum seemed to offer encouragement, with the promise of several exhibits quite clearly labeled *"Homo sapiens."* And I was due to be joined the next day by a fellow-member of this most interesting species.

My friend Doug Powell is a geographer by trade. In other words, he is always probing to find out what makes a place tick—probing among the rocks, the plants, the animals, the people, and the intricate and changing relationships that bind them together. He was therefore expertly qualified to help me interpret whatever I found. He would bring along a piquant bonus too: he is a collateral descendant of the one-armed

John Wesley Powell who in 1869 led the pioneer river passage of Grand Canyon.

And so, on the morning I moved upstream from Beaver Sand Bar, I was pleasantly conscious—perhaps too conscious—that the final two weeks of my journey held high promise of success.

The disturbances began the day after the airdrop.

A note from Doug had come with the drop, confirming that he would join me the following morning. But by noon there was still no sign of him. By four o'clock I was uneasy. By five, fretting. At six, with only two hours of daylight left, I began climbing. A thousand feet above the river I joined the old Tanner Trail, which Doug planned to come down. I had copied the trail's route onto my map from one that illustrated an article by Harvey Butchart in *Appalachia* magazine (that same article I had chanced on soon after my first visit to the Canyon). Harvey had told how a thirty-two-year-old priest and two teen-age boys went down from the Rim to the river one day in July 1959 without registering at a ranger station, then lost their way when climbing back up the trail. Next morning, already desperately dehydrated, they tried to follow a wash back to the river. Soon they came to a sheer eighty-foot drop-off. The priest, apparently irrational by now, had all three take off their shoes and throw them to the bottom. Then he tried to climb down. A few feet, and he fell to his death. The boys soon found a passable route, but one of them died on the way down to the river. The other was rescued by helicopter a week later, eight miles downstream, in critical condition. Harvey had marked his map: PRIEST FELL HERE, and for some reason I had copied the notation onto my own. Now, as I climbed anxiously up the trail, the words leaped out at me each time I glanced at the map.

That evening I climbed only far enough to make sure there were no footprints on the trail, then returned to camp; there is not much you can do about rescue work after dark, especially when you are carrying only a couple of pints of water. Next morning I was walking by six o'clock. My pack held, among other things, first-aid kit, emergency food, and two gallons of water. And I climbed fast: if Doug was in trouble he would not last long without water. Not in the ninety-or-hundred-degree afternoons that every day now generated. As soon as the sun came up, already fiery, I stripped off my clothes.

A thousand feet above the river. Two thousand. Still no footprints. Another glance at the map: PRIEST FELL HERE. Occasionally I was conscious, although worry kept pushing the thought aside, that this new turmoil had already destroyed my peaceful little world of Beaver Sand Bar. I knew, of course, that it would call for everything I had to find Doug, administer first aid if necessary, climb to the Rim for help, and then lead a rescue party down. Yet there was, oddly enough, a moment when I felt a shaft of rather shamefaced pleasure at the prospect of once more having a worthwhile physical challenge to face. I even registered, with some satisfaction, that it showed how completely I had mastered the Canyon's straightforward challenge.

Three hours, and I passed the place the priest and his companions must have lost their way. Soon I was following the trail up through a break in the Redwall. At the top I rested briefly—and found myself looking across at a dry wash that dropped off sheer into a ravine. PRIEST FELL HERE.

Almost three thousand feet above the river now. Only two thousand to the Rim. And still no footprints. I pushed on. The sun swung higher.

Then, quite without warning in that empty and silent place, a voice exclaimed "Colin!" and Doug stood ten paces away at a corner of the trail. His pack was on his back and he looked the very picture of fully hydrated health, even if a shade startled at my décolleté turnout.

We shook hands (somehow it became a curiously formal act, and once again I found myself thinking of Stanley and Livingstone), then sat down on the red rock. Doug had suffered a sharp attack of dysentery the morning he was due to leave the Rim, and there had been no way of letting me know about the delay other than an expensive airdrop. He had started down that morning, as soon as he felt able. It was as simple as that. Two hours later we were back in camp.

But the disturbances were by no means over.

I had camped near the airdrop site, under a rambling sun pavilion of a willow tree. We had hardly been back in its shade for ten minutes when Doug, who was clearing out a place for his sleeping bag under a low horizontal branch, stepped sharply backward.

"Snake!" he said, and pointed.

Stretched out along the branch, passive and amiable, lay a mottled pink rattlesnake, about three feet long. The first Doug had seen of it was a flickering black tongue, six inches from his eyes.

It was a remarkably tolerant creature, that rattlesnake. We pushed it off the branch with a stick so that it fell six feet onto hard sand, and then we harried it with the stick and with waving arms and legs until it retreated into a nearby thicket. Not until just before it disappeared did it adopt a menacing attitude and at last begin to rattle. It had been another gentlemanly meeting. But the next morning soon after breakfast I happened to glance beyond my pack and saw, gliding across the sand, a rattlesnake of very much the same length and color. Slowly the snake threaded its way through a maze of roots. In a patch of dappled sunlight, two feet from my pack, it drew its body into a flat coil, yawned, stretched, laid its head on the pillow of its clean and beautifully marked body, and went to sleep. Because rattlesnakes are undeniably dangerous creatures, and because accidents will happen in the end with even the most amiable of them if they keep coming back, we killed it. The killing was easy; once you've seen a rattlesnake, the poor thing is defenseless. But afterward I could not help remembering how the sleepy animal had yawned and stretched in the dappled sunlight, just as another had yawned and stretched on Beaver Sand Bar. For although the world of Beaver Sand Bar had already slipped back and away out of reach, I could still remember its facts. And I did not like what we had done.

The rattlesnake turned out to be only a beginning.

Doug is a strong, silent type. This is something no one has ever accused me of being, and from the very start I found myself (rather to my surprise) asking for personal news of the outside world.* Almost at once I became stupidly enraged over some small-minded remarks made to Doug by a mutual acquaintance, a man I would have to do business with as soon as I went up out of the Canyon. In normal times I would hardly have given the matter a second thought. But now I fumed, and refused to be extinguished. Looking back later, I think I understood. When you slough off the everyday world, I suppose it is not really surprising that you should lose your armor against its pin-

---

*Later, I learned that Ranger Jim Bailey, on the strength of our meeting at the head of Bass Trail, had warned Doug: "He'll talk your head off for the first day or two, believe me." I would guess that Jim was about right.

pricks and become so sensitive to them that each one feels like a sword thrust of Fate.

After two days we began to move slowly upriver. Now the Canyon itself grew oppressive. The Gorge had widened, shedding its grandeur, becoming less a gorge than a steep and rather forbidding valley. Up and away to the right, the Palisades of the Desert still soared high in echeloned pink cliffs; but that was another world. Down beside the river, deep in the heat, we struggled forward over soft, glaring sand bars. On either side, black lava flows pressed down on us. Above our heads solitary black ravens wheeled and croaked.

The second afternoon we saw two somber sights.

On the last day of June 1956 two transcontinental airliners collided high above the Canyon. Crippled, they plunged to earth, more than a mile apart. There were no survivors. One hundred and twenty-eight people died. That second afternoon we passed the wreckage of both planes. They lay on the far side of the Colorado. All we could see of one of them was a single section of fuselage perched precariously on the brink of a two-thousand-foot cliff. The other plane seemed to have crashed in a shallow sidecanyon, two hundred feet above the river. We could see, strewn across the bare and silent rock, a swathe of small, gleaming fragments. None of them looked larger than a child's coffin. It was a sight that would have lacerated any day. I found that for once I did not want the Canyon's silence. It made it all too easy to hear those last terrible seconds inside the plunging airliner.

We had passed the wreckage and were making our way along a rough and indented terrace, two hundred feet above the river, when the mournful silence was broken in more than vivid imagination. First, a murmur that was barely a tempering of the stillness. Then a hum. Then, suddenly, a roar that echoed among the cliffs. A roar and a distinctive, rhythmic thump. Almost before I had recognized the sound I saw the helicopter.

It was flying at eye level, downriver. We could look across into the ridiculous little glass globule of a cabin and see pilot and passenger sitting side by side in curiously civilized ease. In that somber setting there was something almost indecently public about the sight.

The helicopter cruised slowly past us. The pilot would hardly be expecting to see anyone on the ground, and we would in any case be almost invisible among the dark and jumbled rocks. The machine hovered briefly above the wreckage of the second airliner, then roared and chopped its way back upriver and out of sight. The roar faded, died. But afterward the day belonged even less than before to the Canyon I had come to know.

Late that afternoon we camped on a stony sand bar at the junction of the Little Colorado and the main river. It was not a good camp. But for several days now good camps had been difficult to find. As the afternoons had grown hotter, so their pleasant breezes had become first hostile winds and then blustering gales that whipped dense brown clouds off the sand bars and sent them billowing upriver, downriver, across-river. Wherever we camped, the sand located us. It infiltrated ears, mouth, eyes. It clogged the fine jets of our pressure stoves. It seasoned dinner. Finally, on that sand bar at the mouth of the Little Colorado, it worked its way so deeply and copiously into Doug's camera that the shutter jammed tight. And that mattered.

Doug had compressed his summer schedule very tight. There had barely been time to squeeze in this Canyon trip between a government snow survey in the Sierra Nevada of California and a long-planned visit to an Alaskan glacier. Only after several long-distance calls from Phantom Ranch had I been sure he could come at all; and we had both known all along that he might have to leave the Canyon a little ahead of me. Now the jammed camera threatened all his carefully meshed plans. Glacier photographs were a prime purpose of his Alaskan trip; they would be pivotal in his academic work for a year or more. In addition, the camera was an expensive instrument, not the kind you replace lightly. And he had long ago come to manipulate it without conscious thought—an important factor under adverse field conditions. So after some discussion we decided that, to give him a fair chance of having the camera repaired in time, Doug should leave immediately. We had come barely ten miles upriver, and he would go back out again by the Tanner Trail. As a safety measure, so that Park rangers would know his whereabouts, I would signal the change of plan at the next airdrop, two mornings ahead.

And so, on the sand bar at the mouth of the Little Colorado River, on the fourth day after he had joined me, Doug went back the way we had come.

Frankly, I am sure that we were both distinctly relieved. Under normal conditions Doug and I are liable to find that a casual telephone conversation has escalated to an hour (once, almost unnoticed, to five); yet ever since the moment we met on the Tanner Trail we had failed to communicate. After a couple of days, in frustration at the inability to exchange what was on our minds, we became progressively more irritable—and in the end came close to anger. It sounds ridiculous, I know, but there it was. Looking back later I could see quite clearly that we were speaking from different worlds; and I suspect that things might not have turned out so very differently if it had been the Archangel Gabriel who came down the Tanner Trail. Later, Doug and I agreed that it was singularly blind of us not to have anticipated some such difficulty; but at the time I was in no mood to be sweetly reasonable. All I knew was that I felt frustrated and angry—and that after Doug had gone it was a relief to be able to move on when I wanted to move on, to stand and stare when I wanted to stand and stare, to do absolutely nothing when I wanted to do absolutely nothing. To be able to think my own thoughts in my own way at my own pace and convenience, without fear of interruption. And to exist, all the time, in silence. My relief was not, of course, very surprising. These are exactly the set of circumstances we imply when we use the word "solitude."

It seemed an ironic touch that Doug and I should separate where we did. I had been looking forward for many months to reaching the mouth of the Little Colorado. This was the place that Doug's relative, John Wesley Powell, had considered, almost a hundred years earlier, to mark the real beginning of his passage through Grand Canyon. In his account of the journey he had written:

We are now ready to start on our way down the Great Unknown. Our boats, tied to a common stake, are chafing each other, as they are tossed by the fretful river. They ride high and buoyant, for their loads are lighter than we could desire. We have but a month's rations remaining. . . .

We are three quarters of a mile in the depths of the earth, and the great river shrinks into insignificance, as it dashes its angry waves against the walls and cliffs, that rise to the world above; they are but puny rip-

*ples, and we but pygmies, running up and down the
sands, or lost among the boulders.*

*We have an unknown distance yet to run; an un-
known river yet to explore. What falls there are, we
know not; what walls rise over the river, we know not.
Ah well! we may conjecture many things. The men talk
as cheerfully as ever; jests are bandied about freely
this morning; but to me the cheer is somber and the
jests are ghastly.*

For me, these paragraphs had set the mood of oppression that reverberated through every page of
Powell's report. And long before I came down into the
Canyon I had pictured myself at this junction, looking
back over a hundred years. I am not sure what I hoped
to see. But I know I expected, quite confidently, to feel
at least something of what John Wesley Powell had
felt. I knew, of course, that the shrunken river would
be all wrong, but I felt sure that it would not matter.

Yet now, sitting at the junction, with one Powell
going back the way another had gone forward a hundred years before, I could detect no trace of an echo.
And I knew the river was not the trouble. I knew, wea-
rily, that I would need time now to regain touch, as I
had needed it after Phantom. Time to let the turmoil
fade—the turmoil that had somehow broken in from
the outside world. Time to sink back and down once
more into the silence and the solitude. Time, that is,
to move back inside the museum. And I knew that
with barely a week left before I must begin climbing
out toward the North Rim it was by no means certain
that there were enough silent and solitary days remaining.

From the junction I made a short side-trip up the Little Colorado to the first of the promised exhibits labeled *"Homo sapiens."*

As soon as I moved up into the sidecanyon, the beauty of the place began to calm me. The Little Colorado flows through a narrow, three-thousand-foot gorge, often between strips of thick green foliage. At that time of year it was a gentle stream, heavily mineralized, and its translucent aquamarine water slid and tumbled over white-coated rocks and sand bars. Once, a cluster of crimson flowers overhung a pool. At my feet, in a scene as delicate and pastel-tinted as an Oriental watercolor, a bronze carp cruised pink-finned past a reed bank.

Five miles from the junction I found what I was looking for.

It was a highly improbable object: a brown, smooth-surfaced mound like a huge caramel pudding that had been expertly dunked at the water's edge, upside down, to cool. From a distance it looked, on the floor of that awesome gorge, like a mere pimple. But when I had waded the river I found that around the base it measured more than two hundred feet. I stood looking up perhaps thirty feet to its crest. And when I climbed up onto it I found that the flattened summit was at least forty feet across. In the center of this tableland bubbled a circular yellow pool.

This spring is the mound's creator. I could watch the work still in progress. I could see that, although water kept bubbling up into the pool, none ran out. But I knew that water was continually seeping away under the crusted surface of the tableland and evaporating in the dry air and so building up the mound, crystal by deposited crystal. I knew it for sure because on one flank of the mound I could see the fresh, wet coating, beautifully tinted and exquisitely filigreed, where the main construction happened at this particular moment to be going on.

It is an astonishing place to stand, the tableland-top of that caramel-colored mound. Whichever way you look, your eye meets a beauty that is always startling and sometimes bizarre. The pool, yellow and foam-flecked. The crusted surface of the tableland, pink-brown and smooth, but here and there cracked and flaking. The darker flanks of the mound, crumbling into rubble. Below, the translucent river. Sand bars, pale and glaring. Foliage, dark and comforting. Above, a strip of buff-colored cliff-and-talus, battlemented, barely two hundred feet high. Then the Redwall. And then cliff after terrace after cliff reaching up and up, red and then pink and then white, until the rock cuts off at last and your eye halts against distant blue sky.

And yet, in spite of the beauty and the silence and the solitude regained, I did not really find what I had come for.

In my mind, this natural but very unnatural-looking mound was clearly labeled *"Homo sapiens"* because it was a religious shrine. The bubbling hot spring on its summit is to the Hopi Indians a Sipapu (pronounced "seep-a-*pooh*"), "A place at which life has issued forth from the earth." And the Hopi people believe that this mound beside the Little Colorado is the place—or at least one of the places—that their primeval ancestors emerged from the earth. In the beginning this explanation must have answered in a new and exciting and crystal-clear way the conundrum that has always haunted us men: "Where do we come from?" Must have answered it, for the developing minds of a simple people, with satisfying certainty. With the same kind of certainty with which the unfolding story of the rocks and fossils is now answering it for our own developing and still simple minds.

As I stood beside the bubbling spring I tried to project myself into the mind of the Hopi who discovered the Sipapu. (For obvious but quite illogical reasons, I pictured the discovery being made by one man, alone.) But my attempt never developed beyond an empty intellectual exercise. I could tell myself easily enough that this man would undoubtedly be apprehensive after many miles of travel in a strange place, deep in the earth, far below the mesas that were his home. I could even construct thin thoughts about the awe he must have felt and the excited story he would carry back to his people. But that was all. I failed completely to move "inside" him as I had been able to move inside the beaver and the rattlesnake and even the sandfly on Beaver Sand Bar. I had not met this man, of course. But then I had not meet the coyote or the mountain lion either; and I had felt, more than intellectually, at least the fringes of what they felt.

I retreated from the sun-scorched tableland and sat under some bushes and looked at the mound and tried to fit it into the history of its setting.

I saw clearly enough that on the time scale of the rocks that towered above it the mound had barely begun to exist. It had begun to grow, layer on layer, so long after the creation of even the youngest of the rocks that from their point of view it had appeared at virtually the split second I set eyes on it.

Even on the time scale of the gorge in which it stood the mound was young. The Little Colorado had presumably, like the main river, taken about seven million years to excavate its canyon. Three thousand feet in seven million years. I took out my notebook and played with figures: four feet in ten thousand years.

It was clear that the mound in its present form could only have begun to grow when the floor of the canyon reached roughly its present level. No more, perhaps, than fifty thousand years ago.

But on the time scale we humans customarily use the mound was old. Very old. I had no way of judging how long ago that pioneering Hopi ventured down into the gorge. A fair guess seemed to be somewhere around a thousand years, but it made little difference if the figure turned out to be two thousand, or even three: on our human scale, the mound was still so old that the word "growth" became almost meaningless. If that long-dead Hopi had materialized beside me as I sat under the bushes looking out at the huge brown shape he would probably have noticed no change in its outline.

There under the bushes, these thoughts seemed both interesting and instructive. But when I stood up at last and walked down to the water's edge and took off my boots and waded back across the beautiful pale blue river, I knew that they too had been a mere intellectual exercise. And afterward, as I walked downstream toward the junction, striding out along pale sand bars in the heat of the afternoon, I knew, disconsolately, that if I had visited the Sipapu a week earlier the day would have held different and deeper meanings.

Next day I moved on up the main river. Even before I left the junction I knew that the next twenty-four hours would do very little to help calm me. They would hold me tight to the thin and immediate present.

At the very start I had to tackle the one big physical challenge that was left: in order to reach the final airdrop site and my exit route, I had to swim across the Colorado.

I chose a crossing place barely half a mile above the Little Colorado—a slow-moving stretch of river, several hundred yards above any rapids. I knew that the dam-emasculated Colorado flowing quietly past me bore almost no relation to the swirling, plunging torrent that had drowned at least seventeen or eighteen men within the Canyon, including a companion of Harvey Butchart's who in May 1955 was swept off his air mattress by a whirlpool, grabbed the mattress, and was rolled under. But the knowledge did not do me much good. I still stripped off my clothes very slowly and stowed everything away in my pack bag even more slowly, making a big inner envelope around almost all the gear with the white plastic sheet that had wrapped everything on the Havasu Creek reconnaissance. Then I made a couple of procrastinating trial swims out into the current without the pack. But at last there was nothing for it but to sling the pack over one shoulder and lie across the little green air mattress and push myself out into the broad expanse of river.

It was almost an anticlimax. The pack stayed neatly balanced between buttock and bald patch, the way I had learned to hold it on the short buttress detours below Beaver Sand Bar. My head stayed pointing toward the far bank. The staff floated clear and unencumbering at the end of its three-foot nylon cord. And although there was an epoch out in the middle of the river when it seemed that my steady dog-paddling had ceased to move me forward, the feeling of helplessness passed. So, after a little while, did the tiredness of tensed muscles. And in due time I came easily in under the far bank. I let a backwater carry me a few feet upstream to a sandy beach. My toes touched bottom. And then—dripping mattress clasped to dripping body, staff still trailing out behind—I was climbing up the soft, sloping sand, almost exactly opposite the place I had started.

The warm afterglow of success that spread through mind and body as I sat and let the sun towel me dry was a tame thing compared with the flood of elation that had surged up six weeks before as I clambered onto the beach on the far side of the Havasu back eddy. And even this mild glow failed to last. As I hurried upriver, rockledge and sand bar for five miles, it slowly faded away. When I camped that evening at the mouth of Kwagunt Creek, only a ghost remained. And by next morning even the ghost had gone.

That morning I took my third and final airdrop. It did nothing to soothe me.

The drop site was the open delta of Kwagunt Creek; zero hour, ten o'clock. By nine fifteen, with the June sun already beating fiercely down, I had spread out the big white plastic sheet as identification marker and had boot-scraped my message in five-foot letters on the gravelly soil of the delta: DOUG DUE OUT TANNER 9TH. But the result hardly looked clear enough, and I began to reinforce the more important letters of the message with toilet paper. And then, when a light breeze sprang up, to thumb tack the toilet paper in place with prickly-pear stems. And then, when I ran out of toilet paper, to use the precious white onion-skin sheets reserved for my notes. And then, with these finished too and time suddenly running very short, to press into service every plastic bag, prickly-pear stem, and light-colored rock I could lay hurried hands on. I finished at two minutes to ten, breathless and exhausted.

The plane was an hour late. By the time it appeared at last, droning along high up near the Rim, I had fretted myself into the kind of state that lies beyond the reach of all but natural-born worriers.

The little Cessna made four runs: Doug's food; then a can of white gas; then my food; and then a check run to see that all was well. On each run the plane passed barely a hundred and fifty feet above me. Against the background of towering red cliffs it looked very puny and very fragile. On the final run it acknowledged my message with an unmistakable rock of the wings. Then it was gone, and the silence had moved softly in behind it.

For a day and a half after the airdrop I sat and rested—because of a cut foot that had become mildly infected—in a willow thicket beside the Colorado.

At first I remained acutely conscious that the disturbances were still churning around inside me. But my camp among the willows, with the white plastic sheet now strung up as an awning, was a pleasant place, and as the hours passed the Canyon began its quiet work.

It was good, I found, to look up and out past the awning, through a screen of willow shoots, and study without haste the sculpture of the gorge. Here, the Redwall dominated. It soared up clean and sheer from close to the water's edge. Above, more cliffs. And then the sky. That was all. It was very simple and very beautiful. And now I had time to fix the beauty on my memory so that I could carry it away into the days beyond the Canyon.

You need catalytic moments to fix really lasting beauty. And they came.

Morning. Sunlight cutting every object knife-edge sharp. The mirror surface of the Colorado shattering over into rapids. And then the day crystallizing, almost behind my back, to its brief but electric desert climax.

Night. The soft, slipping sound of the river. Shimmering reflections of red rock. High above, in the dying moonlight, huge shapes already sinking down through blue to black. Far upriver, the source of the red reflection: a huge rock buttress, still luminous. A buttress glowing like a stained-glass window in the last pale sunlight of a winter's evening. A stained-glass window very far away—and I a very small child at the door of a long, cool, dimly lit cathedral.

Once, at dusk, I heard the distant double-stone explosion of a slapping beaver tail. And once, in midafternoon, a hummingbird materialized eighteen inches from my nose, startling, violet, iridescent. The quivering little bundle inspected and rejected, in brisk and efficient rotation, pink toothbrush, red socks, and red plastic canteen top. It hovered before the can of white gas; touched, with exquisite gentleness, the red shirt of a figure painted on the can; and then, finding it had been deceived, up-tailed and dematerialized.

My second afternoon among the willows brought an unexpected moment that seemed at first like another disturbance. I was sitting reading. It was very hot, even under my awning. All at once, out of the heat and the silence, from somewhere upriver, building in an instant from murmur to thunder, grew a roar that made me think, in the seconds left before its climax: "Why, that sounds just like a couple of jets coming through low! But of course it can't be." I lifted the edge of my awning and pushed aside the screen of willow stems. And there directly in front of me I saw, startlingly close, hurtling past at half the height the little Cessna had flown and at five times its speed, two silvery jet fighters. For a moment I was staring, astonished, at riveted plates and big black numbers. Then the planes had flashed by, fifty feet apart, and were gone. Their tumult subsided, echoed, died.

I let my screen of willow stems spring shut. For a long time I sat wondering what was wrong with the way I felt. I knew exactly what I should have been feeling. I should have been deploring with self-righteous fervor what these two pilots had done. They had broken National Park rules, good, sensible, badly needed rules. They were frightening wild animals. They were threatening to topple loose rocks. Above all, they had shattered the silence. My silence. Yes, I should have been deploring, all right.

Instead, all I could feel was admiration. Admiration for their skill, their damned-fool daring, and their courage. And that, whether I liked it or not, was no disturbance. Rather the reverse, in fact.

Next day I went pottery-hunting.

Just before the airdrop I had, quite by accident, unearthed two pieces of blue-gray pottery as I boot-scraped the o of DOUG. During the long hour's wait for the plane I had scuffed away a bit more, rather absent-mindedly, and had soon found four more fragments. I had put them on one side, on a big stone. And on the second morning after the airdrop I went back to the delta and began scraping again.

Almost at once I found more fragments near the o of DOUG. Then, off to one side, several more. Most of the pieces were quite small, but a few measured four or five inches across. There were three quite distinct types of pottery. The most common kind was blue-gray. Its inside surfaces had been finished smooth. But the outsides were covered with an ornamental pattern of overlapping layers about half an inch wide, running parallel to the rim, as if the vessels had been built up on a coil system. The edges of these layers had been carefully crimped, apparently with finger and thumb, much as a pastry cook crimps a pie edge. Another kind of pottery was dark red. Its surfaces, both of them smooth, had a slightly polished finish. And the outside surfaces of many fragments had been painted with bold black lines that seemed to be part of quite complicated decorative designs. The third kind of pottery was similar, but white.

As I scraped away in the loose soil of the delta, gradually moving further and further from the o of DOUG, I began to find flints too, both arrowheads and rounded scraper-flints. And then I found the ghosts of two houses. At one site, lines of stones clearly marked three side walls. The other house was a mere depression in the ground, quite shallow. But the depression formed an undeniable square. And that, without question, meant "man." For Nature did not generate a straight line, let alone a square (not on this sort of scale, anyway), until she produced man, and quite modern man at that.

All morning and most of the afternoon I scraped away in the delta and collected and washed and photographed many pieces of pottery and flint. (I carried nothing away; the whole object of a National Park is the protection of its treasures.) But in the evening, when I had time to disengage myself from the activities themselves and to stand back and evaluate them, I saw that it all added up to very little. Very little indeed. I had not even glimpsed a new gallery of my museum. I had not begun to move inside the people who once lived on the delta. Had not even begun to bring them alive.

The day had not been wasted, though. It had brought a long-simmering idea to the boil. And early next morning I wrapped half a day's food and some photographic equipment in my poncho, tied the bundle to the back of my waist belt, clipped a canteen onto the belt, and headed up Kwagunt Creek.

During the year that separated decision from journey I had read about a park ranger who thirty-five years earlier had reported finding a "fifty-room Indian village" in Kwagunt Basin. It seemed that no one had ever rediscovered the village, or even seen a trace of it from the air.

The story had intrigued me. And one evening, months before I came down into the Canyon, I was indulging in the delightful, time-wasting vice of map-brooding when I found myself trying to figure out where an Indian community, settling down for some reason in Kwagunt Basin, would build their village. They would want water close by. And protection from flash floods. And a piece of reasonably level ground that was easy to cultivate and to defend against enemies. In the end—knowing perfectly well that the chances were all against there being time for me to make a side trip up Kwagunt Creek and check the results of my little game—I selected what seemed the two most likely sites, circled them on the map in pencil, smiled, and more or less forgot the whole thing. But once your curiosity has been piqued you are never safe. (At least, if you are, then God help you.) And ever since I came down into the Canyon the whimsical fifty-room-village notion had simmered away somewhere in the back of my mind. On Beaver Sand Bar, when I began to think of exhibits marked *"Homo sapiens,"* I had tentatively decided to make the side trip into Kwagunt Basin. And once I found the pottery and ghost houses at the mouth of the creek, I was sure about it.

Two miles above the delta I came out of the narrow canyon through which Kwagunt Creek flows just before it empties into the Colorado, and in front of me there opened up the huge expanse of Kwagunt Basin. Its stark hills and ridges rolled back mile after mile to the foot of hazy cliffs that formed the North Rim of the Canyon. It looked at first glance like the sort of place you could tuck a five-hundred-room village into and still keep your secret. And as I walked up into the silent, intimidating basin I also had to admit to myself that it did not really look the sort of place anyone would choose to establish a village in. But at least Kwagunt Creek now flowed on the surface, which was more than it had done down near the delta. And a village would certainly need water.

Two hours after leaving camp I arrived at the foot of a low, steep bluff on the north bank of the creek. At the top of this bluff lay the little plateau, or flat, that I had picked from the map as my first-choice village site.

The bluff was very steep, and as I scrambled up it I thought, smugly, that at least I had been right when I looked at the map a year earlier and guessed that it would make an excellent defensive flank for any village on the plateau above.

A hundred feet above the creek I came to the crest of the bluff. And in the first moment I stood on the plateau I saw, barely a dozen paces ahead, clearly visible in the low and widely spaced scrub, a line of large stones. I knew at once, though I hardly dared believe it, that they might have been put there by man. Six strides, and the outline was unmistakable. Three strides more and I could even see, near one corner of the nine-by-eighteen-foot rectangle, the gap that had been the doorway.

But I still did not know how old the house was: it might have been the home of some quite recent prospector like William Bass. I walked a few yards up the flat. Almost at once, in the lee of a big limestone boulder, another rectangular outline. I turned and walked down past the first house to the point of the flat. It was there, all right, just as I had felt sure it would be in any kind of a village: another rectangle of stones standing guard over the approach up the creek. Almost at once, near one corner of the house, a fragment of pottery caught my eye. It was blue-gray. I picked it up. It bore the same crimped, pastry-cook pattern as the fragments I had found down on the delta.

It was a satisfying moment. Perhaps it amounted to nothing more, really, than bumptious self-satisfaction at having map-read my way into the minds of some long-dead Indians. But I knew that as I stood looking up and across the scrub-covered flat, with the little fragments of pottery clutched in my hand, the day was suddenly rounder and fuller than any day had been since Beaver Sand Bar.

Eagerly, I walked up the flat past the other two stone outlines. Soon, beyond a slight rise, the outline of a fourth house. A bigger house, thirty feet square. And when I walked around to its far side I found the stone foundations of a little annex, a sort of tacked-on afterthought of a room, with no doorway linking it to the main house. I stood beside this little annex and looked ahead, out over the open flat. There was quite obviously space to spare for another forty-five rooms.

For the next half hour I traversed steadily across the flat from one side to the other, tracing a pattern tight enough to make reasonably sure I missed not even the faintest outline of stones. When I finished the census my room total had risen by exactly zero.

It was, I must admit, a disappointment. And perhaps that was part of the reason I did not explore my second-choice village site, a mile further on. Or perhaps it was just that when I looked up and across the deeply eroded valley floor it seemed a long and weary trudge to make in the heat of the day. Anyway, I stayed where I was and settled down to pottery-hunting.

I spent most of the day at it. I found plenty of fragments, and all of them belonged to one of the three types I had found at the delta. I carefully collected, washed, laid out and photographed the best pottery fragments and the finest flint arrowheads. As on the delta, it seemed to be something I ought to do, for the record; but I must admit that, after the first excitement of discovery, a reaction had set in. The highlight of the afternoon, really, was a magnificent eight- or ten-point buck, still in velvet, that scrambled to its feet barely thirty yards from me and then retreated quite slowly, with much snorting and considerable dignity, as if registering a protest against upstart trespassers.

About six o'clock I started, rather disconsolately, back for camp.

I had walked less than halfway when it occurred to me for no apparent reason that although I had not found a fifty-room village my hamlet could at a pinch be called a five-room village; and that the disparity could just conceivably have arisen through a simple clerical error in copying out the figures in a ranger's report.

This rather farfetched explanation, justified or not, made a difference.*

---

*Many months later I learned that the explanation, although not justified in quite the sense I intended, was not so very farfetched after all. The original report had indeed been garbled. But it fell victim not to clerical error but to the human flair for exaggeration.

The literature on Grand Canyon contains several references to this "fifty-room village." One of them had triggered my little map game. But I finally discovered that the original report, made by a Park Naturalist in December 1928, reads: "When we reached camp Ranger Brown announced the discovery of a 'lost city' containing at least twenty-five rooms. He discovered several pictographs under a ledge and collected a flint skinning knife, several arrowheads, and pieces of flint."

According to an anthropologist who has explored Kwagunt Basin fairly

It made a difference, I mean, to my mood. By the time I reached camp I knew that, in spite of the disappointment, the day had been decidedly worthwhile. It had been a great deal better, certainly, than any day since Beaver Sand Bar. After all, the fifty-room-village game had only been, as is usually the way with games, an excuse. What mattered was that I had, almost without knowing it, begun groping toward an understanding of "my people." (It seems an odd conceit, I know, to speak of "my people," but that is the way I already thought of these ancient Indians who had once lived on bluff and delta. You become quite absurdly possessive, I find, out on your own.)

I had gleaned, of course, no facts about my people. And for once my decision not to read up on the Canyon beforehand was a decided drawback. I did not even know the traditional uses that anthropologists had no doubt assigned by now to the three different kinds of pottery. But in two days of moving over ground that was once my people's ground I had collected a grab bag of tenuous insights into their ways of thinking. I had confirmed, for example, that they were highly flood-conscious: both their house sites stood on raised ground, inconveniently far from water but safely clear of flash floods (though they no doubt chose both sites in part because the ground was extremely flat, and therefore suitable for cultivation). I surmised that they paid little attention to the sun's heat: the houses faced in a variety of directions, and none stood in any kind of shade (though if they made use of or planted trees, these might by now have vanished). Most important, perhaps, I had glimpsed their sense of beauty. To us, piecrust crimpings and crudely

---

extensively since my visit, it seems highly improbable that any "lost city" exists; only some "relatively small pueblo sites, from one to a dozen rooms."

painted black lines may seem rather rudimentary art; but then, our artistic efforts will certainly seem rudimentary to our successors.

There had been one moment that half promised something more.

Beside the largest house in the basin settlement I had sat looking down at a red, ripple-marked slab of limestone that had once formed a part of the house wall. And I found myself wondering what my people had made of these raised markings. They would hardly explain them, I decided, as the time-cemented impressions of a rippling sea that once covered what was now Kwagunt Basin. More likely, they did what men have always found necessary, and still do, when they discover a yawning chasm out beyond the boundaries of their knowledge: they invoked legend and purple myth, resonant with half-glimpsed truth.

But even this moment of promise, tentative and ill-focused as it was, had not lasted. The rest of the day, hour after hour, I had looked at the arrowheads and the pottery as interesting relics, not as the very personal belongings of warm, pulsing people. I had not seen the arrowheads as the cared-for weapons that a hungry man had taken with him long ago, when he set off up Kwagunt Creek to hunt—perhaps even to hunt the ancestors of the dignified ten-pointer I had seen. I had not looked at the fragments of pottery as if some of them had come—as it was possible to imagine— from a vessel that some hard-working housewife had hauled up from the creek, full and heavy, on sinewy shoulders. A vessel she had filled and poured from and refilled so often that, unknowing, she knew by heart its every chip and indentation.

The village, in other words, had not been Beaver Sand Bar.

But it had been a beginning. And after dinner that

night, as I studied the map in the small bright pool of my flashlight beam, I found myself looking repeatedly at an odd little symbol near the mouth of Nankoweap Creek. It was labeled "Cliff Dwellings." The words had been intriguing me for almost a year; and now, with Nankoweap Creek barely four miles ahead and with my mind still brooding over the way I had failed to move "inside" my people, a simple and obvious thought occurred to me: "If you want to know how a cliff dweller felt, go dwell in his cliff." And before I fell asleep, lulled by soft river sounds, I understood that I had one final chance to move back inside my museum.

I left my willow thicket camp late next day, in the cool of evening, and for the first time since I went up the Tanner Trail to look for Doug I found myself relaxed and at peace. Dusk was already creeping down into the Gorge; yet as I walked easily upriver along the sand bars and rockledges everything I looked at seemed to stand out sharp and clear. On one sand bar, many square yards of its damp surface had been so pockmarked with the fretwork of tiny feet that I could almost see the busy brown mice scurrying and scraping and nibbling away their white-footed, light-footed night. On another sand bar, a carp dashed off in alarm at my approach, creating a brown swirl in the tiny bay in which it had been lying. The swirl brought down a miniature avalanche from the sandy, six-inch "cliff face" of the bay, and at once I saw the event as another link in those little chains of chance that hasten the huge and inevitable process of erosion—the kind of minuscule event that causes, in colossal aggregation, a phenomenon like Grand Canyon.

Once, as I eased along a rockledge, a familiar "ker-PLOOSH." A lesser explosion this time, but unmistakable. Almost at once, gliding diagonally across the current, a brown shape. I halted. The beaver came on, eighteen-inch-long body riding high. The sleek and shining little animal cruised past, then stopped beside a small mound of half-floating branches. Very slowly, I moved forward. At last I stood directly above the den. The beaver lay still, looking up at me. And there in the gray dusk we remained, both of us motionless, both of us quite plainly fascinated by what we saw. After a long, long time the beaver paddled gently forward. For a moment it seemed to be nosing at some of the branches. Then came a quiet folding of the water's surface, an almost imperceptible healing-over where something had been, and I was alone.

I camped soon afterward, on a sand bar. I camped at the very edge of the slipping, lapping river. And I lit no fire. I wanted to be alone, now, with the darkness. With the sounds and the silence and the shapes and the stars.

It was in this happy and included state of mind that I came next morning to the mouth of Nankoweap Creek.

They were there, all right: three small caves in the face of the Redwall, six hundred feet above the river. The leftmost cave was just a small, dark patch. In the center cave stood an unnaturally angular, boxlike shape, the same shade of pink as the surrounding rock. But the third cave was the one. Its mouth was blocked by a curving pink wall; and set in this wall were three small window openings—black, rectangular, and tantalizing.

As soon as I had filled all my canteens from the river I struck away from it toward the gray-green talus that slanted steeply up to the foot of the Redwall.

From a distance the talus looked appallingly steep. And the few feet of sheer rock that separated the top of it from the caves seemed quite unclimbable. But the talus turned out to be a very simple scramble. And although I found, close up, that the "few feet of sheer rock" above it had stretched as usual to forty feet, I also found that it had, just as predictably, coarsened into substantial and easily climbed ledges. Half an hour after leaving the river I stepped up into the mouth of the right-hand cave. As I did so I turned so that I was half-facing outward—into a world of astonishing space and light.

The space opened out and away from the rock in every direction, free and boundless. The distant cliffs and terraces quite failed in their feeble attempts to limit it. And the whole of this huge space glowed with a soft and luminous light—the same soft and luminous light I remembered from my first moment of shock on the Rim of the Canyon. The light penetrated every corner of the space. It even seemed to penetrate the distant, feeble cliffs.

It was a totally unexpected world. Down below, I had thought of "my man the cave dweller" as a timid, penned-in creature, cowering in constant fear of his enemies. But I had forgotten the solace and then the strength you can draw from high places. And now that I had reached my man's home I understood, beyond the shadow of a doubt, that he was a proud and erect individual. A man with a consciousness of power and domain. In such a place it could not have been otherwise. And when I turned away at last from the space and the light and let my eye run down the little line of rooms, from window to window, I knew that when this man let his eye run down, as mine had just done, from window to window, he sometimes thought "This is home!" and felt the swelling pride of possession.

I took off my pack and inspected our establishment.
The cave turned out to be not so much a cave, really,
as a moderately deep ledge tucked in under a massive
protecting overhang.*

The wall that blocked off the rear part of this natural ledge-cave had been built with flat, carefully laid
pieces of limestone bound together by some kind of
mud-plaster. Stonework and mud were both the same
cheerful pink as the surrounding rock. Let into this
wall were four window-doorways (from below, one
had been hidden). Each opening served one very small
chamber, and each chamber was partitioned off from
its neighbor. A couple of ledges down and a few feet
off to one side there jutted out from the cliff face the
three-sided remains of another room. Perhaps, I
thought, this was the kitchen. I failed, though, to find
any sign of fire marks.

Presently I traversed out along the cliff face on a
narrow ledge. The boxlike shape in the center cave
turned out to be another small stone-and-plaster
room. The farthest cave ran back fifteen or twenty
feet into solid rock. Two faint outlines on the floor
suggested that flimsy, small-man-sized mudwork
structures had been built against its walls. Near the

---

*The caves did not cut back, as I had thought, into the face of the Red-
wall. They stood at its very base, between the unfractured limestone of the
Redwall and the bedded Muav limestone that underlies it throughout the
Canyon. To an eye as geologically unsubtle as mine, the Muav tends to
merge with the similarly colored rock above (though there is actually a
massive unconformity between them, representing a gap of 150 million
years). When I looked up at the caves from the river I had made my usual
mistake. But now, close up, I could see that the rock ledges above the talus
had been eroded from the stratified Muav. Only the solid overhang was
Redwall.

Looking at the cliff dwellings in this light, it occurred to me that Frank
Lloyd Wright would have approved of the way my man had meshed his
home with the natural features of the landscape; but I doubted that my
man would have known what the hell the eminent architect was talking
about.

This is known as progress. And I guess it is.

rear of the cave, perfectly preserved in that dim, dry place where direct sunlight never penetrated, I found two crude wooden "chopsticks," one of them charred at one end, and the stripped-off inner stalks of several very small corncobs. Otherwise the place was bare.

I climbed back to my pink apartment house, unpacked, and settled in.

Of the four little rooms, one of the center pair was so small that I felt sure it had been built for a child. The other, rather less cramped, looked as though it might have done for a reasonably petite wife. The two end chambers were bigger, and the farthest offered not only the widest part of the ledge as its front porch but also a jutting section of wall that created a little alcove—the sort of useful place in which any present-day man would unhesitatingly dump his traveling bag when he had unpacked. I designated this farthest chamber the "master cubicle."

When I had first looked inside the cubicle I had thought: "What tiny people they must have been!" Yet when I crawled in through the doorway and stretched out full length I found that there was plenty of room for my hundred-and-eighty-pound bulk. The cubicle showed every sign of having been built for a man just about my size. Its floor measured three feet by seven. The roof, at the point I needed to sit up, seemed to have been chipped away to give a convenient three-foot clearance.

Once I had grown used to the gloom and a slight stuffiness, I decided that my master bedroom was a distinctly comfortable place. It offered advantages that would roll easily off any realtor's tongue. It was cool, and quite free from the usual desert dust. And its picture doorway commanded, beyond the blue-and-white river, a breath-stopping sweep of curved rock—

a view that would have added thousands of dollars to the value of any house built today.*

I dwelt in my cliff dwelling for twenty-four hours. And, hour by hour—conscious of my vast ignorance, yet curiously confident—I began to focus my cave dweller more sharply.

First I pictured him building his home. I saw him chipping patiently away at the roof of the cave, so that there would be headroom when he sat up in his cubicle. (If I was right in assuming that he had built this cubicle to fit his own person—and at the time I had no doubts at all—then he was a shade shorter than I am, butt to crown, though only by a bare inch.) I saw him chipping back the footwall at an angle, so as to make room for his legs. I saw him, next, choosing with unhurried care the material for the cubicle walls. I saw him cementing each piece of rock in place with pink mud-plaster that he had probably made from pounded rock. I saw him nod with satisfaction when, after fitting several oversize pieces near the place his head would come, he lay down full length and found, sure enough, that the protrusions formed neat little ledges in exactly the right convenient place for whatever he wanted handy little ledges for. (Not pen and notebook, like me, of course; but he wanted

*At the time I was distinctly vague about when the cliff dwellings had been built, but soon after I came out of the Canyon an anthropologist at the Museum of Northern Arizona told me that my cliff dwellers—who were apparently the same people as my house dwellers—used the Nankoweap site as recently as A.D. 1200.

The anthropologist also told me that expert opinion presently regards these cliff dwellings as having been built as storage rooms (or granaries), though they may have been used from time to time as habitations. But I must confess that, having assumed all along that they were indeed dwellings, and having so recently seen how they appeared to have been built with considerable care to accommodate the human frame, I found this conclusion difficult to swallow. Frankly, standing foursquare on my base of open-minded ignorance, I still do. I would accept, perhaps, that my people may have lived in the cliff dwellings only in bad weather or when enemies threatened, but that is as far as I am presently willing to retreat.

them for something, all right.) I saw him fashioning the doorway: neatly rectangular and just big enough for him to pass through once he had learned the proper jackknife technique (which I soon did). I saw him, next, making the door lintel: peeling the bark off a stick about an inch in diameter and three feet long, smoothing off its undersurface, and squaring off one side for about nine inches at each end so that when he cemented the stick in position it could not rotate. (Like most natural sticks, it was not quite straight, and if it had been free to rotate it would not have done its job.) Finally I saw my satisfied craftsman jackknifing through the doorway to make sure that the stick was in exactly the right position to warn him, by touching his bent back, that if he straightened a half inch more he would break the stick and the rough stone above the doorway would gouge into his bare skin. I found myself wishing he could have known that thanks to his meticulous work this same stick, protected from rain and direct sunlight and practically indestructible in such a dry climate, would also be brushing my back in timely warning, all these years further down the line.*

I slept soundly through a warm night. Then it was day again. And as the hours passed I came to feel that slowly—not through conscious effort, but merely by living as he had lived—I was coming to know a little more about this man who had preceded me. Piece by untidily added piece, I explored new sectors of the life

---

*At the time I had no doubt at all that this was the stick's function. I still think it was; but I am less sure. It may be that what my man made so carefully was a curtain rod. Perhaps reeds hung from the stick, or beads on some kind of string. I doubt it, though: the empty doorway was a tight enough fit, even allowing for my man's undoubtedly superior agility.

Some anthropologists apparently regard the sticks as mere supporting units for strengthening the stone-and-plaster structure. But I am afraid I simply cannot bring myself to accept this contention. The sticks are frail, and quite superficially attached. The walls are very strong.

he had led. Or at least that I confidently imagined he had led.

It seemed reasonable to assume that fear of enemies had driven him up into the cliff. No other reason, in fact, made much sense. And he had chosen a superb defensive position. His rear and flanks were impregnable. And any frontal attack would smack of suicide. In daylight, enemies could approach no closer than the foot of the talus, six hundred feet below, without being seen. And as soon as they began to scramble up the talus they became vulnerable to rolled rocks and thrown stones as well as plunging arrows. If the attackers managed to climb close enough to retaliate, the small doorways of the cubicles would protect the cowering women and children. Even the men, hurling rocks or firing arrows, would be quite well protected by the lip of the ledge. And in the final savage moments the defenders would hold every advantage as they swung their long clubs and as a last desperate resort kicked and punched at the breathless, precariously balanced invaders.

At night, the dice were hardly less loaded. Any intruder had to climb the last forty feet on small ledges he had never seen. And if he succeeded in creeping up to the first cubicle (which had a neat peephole overlooking the only approach) without awakening anyone (assuming that the family ever slept *en bloc*), he still had to make a mortal thrust through the small doorway before any kind of startled, clumsy push sent him cartwheeling back the way he had come, screaming and doomed.

Day or night, there was precious little doubt whose side I would rather be on.*

---

*An obvious objection to the defensive situation I have outlined is one that frankly did not occur to me at the time: that attackers had only to sit down and wait for the defenders to run out of water. But to my relief the

In time of danger there would naturally be fear as
you waited. But there always is, in any kind of war-
fare. And that unoutflankable ledge did not seem too
bad a place to be frightened in, especially if you were
squatting there with a comfortable stock of boulders
poised ready to roll, and a mound of sling-size stones,
and a bow and flint-headed arrows, and, as final re-
serve, a long and trusty club close at hand and held
fast by stones to keep it from rolling down and away.
A better place to be frightened in than a World War
II pillbox, certainly. An incomparably better place
than somewhere deep and anonymous with the firing
button of an ICBM under your metaphorical thumb
as you waited, waited, waited to be told at the hun-
dredth remove that some distant member of the same
demented species had just pushed his own terrible
and impersonal button.

During my stay in the cliff dwelling I also kept company with my man in a few of his peaceful leisure
moments and learned some of the little, important
things. I sat as he must often have sat, doing nothing
in particular, outside his cubicle door. My bare butt
occupied the same convenient little squatting-ledge
that his must have occupied. My toes curled over the
same rough lip of rock that his had curled over. My
eyes saw what his had seen: river, rock, sky, space,
and luminous light. My ears heard what his heard:
silence; the roar of the river; the repetitive but liquid
call of a rock wren; the tearing of air as a swift
plunged past; the mewing of two hawks that had made
their home in the cliff face, a hundred feet higher than

---

anthropologist I consulted on this point did not find the objection valid.
He seemed to accept that attackers would be very small bands of marauders passing through the territory. Even if these marauders wanted to lay
siege to the cliff dwellings—which was not apparently the accepted pattern
of things—they would have to find food to subsist on. And that would be
no easy task in such inhospitable country.

his. ("Were there really hawks nesting up above in his time?" I wondered.)

By now I had picked up some other facts too. I had discovered that bare feet are remarkably safe engines to use for climbing around on loose rock. Also that my man's soles were tougher than mine. I learned that when he belched, it echoed. And, when, following up this revelation, I lay in our little cubicle and called out to his wife through the partition, I confirmed that we lived—he and I—in a natural echo chamber.

There was one thing about the life of this man and his wife that I understood more clearly now than I had done in the beginning. The first time I looked inside the master cubicle I had thought not only what small people the occupants must have been but also how difficult it must be to beget children in such cramped quarters. After I had spent a night in the cubicle I knew better. There was plenty of room. It was a warm place too, and snugly private. You could do much worse.

Many details of my cliff dweller's domestic life still puzzled me, of course. The family no doubt tossed their garbage down the cliff. But what, I wondered, about toilet arrangements? And there was also the problem of how to keep the kids from falling downstairs.*

Many such surface details of my man's life remained a blank. But in the course of the second morning I began to feel that I was learning things of a quite different kind.

---

*When I raised this question with one anthropologist he said: "Oh, that's easy. Go and watch the Hopi families. They live on high mesas, and their children play quite freely close to cliff tops. Safety is a communal affair. The older children learn to keep a strict eye on the younger ones until they have learned to look after themselves. The system works."

With plenty of children, I'm sure it works. But it seems to me that my one-family—or at most, two-family—residence might have been rather lightly populated for such a neat and practical solution.

It seemed clear to me by then that my man was blessed with an insight that we modern men tend to lose, walled in as we are by our complexities (or do I mean walled *out?*). Living his simple life—eating breakfast with his wife and children on the ledge, watching the swifts plunge past and snap up their insect breakfasts, watching the hawks come mewing back to their upper-story home with breakfasts for *their* children—he could hardly help but understand, clearly and steadily, that man is an integral part of everything that goes on around him. More particularly, because the rock was a part of everything he did—sitting, seeing, hearing, cooking, fighting, making love—he understood it. Naturally, his understanding was different from mine. Even his questions were different. When he lay in our master cubicle and looked up at the chipped gray limestone above his head—at the same chip marks that I looked up at—he probably did not wonder why the rock was gray inside and red on its surface. He almost certainly did not conclude that it was stained by long ages of rainwater from the red rocks above. And yet (it seemed contradictory at first, but I don't think it really was) I felt that he knew something about the rhythm of the rocks. Not in a logical way, of course, that he could have talked about. But I had an idea that when he looked at a partly detached slab of pink rock down near the kitchen and wondered how long before it would fall, he would have known in his own way that it would still be standing partly detached when I passed by, centuries later, to take his place for a day and a night.

Because this man lived in a different age, the surface of his answers would clearly be different from mine. He could not ponder on the marvel and mystery of a Redwall that had been built by the remains of countless tiny organisms that are in a tenuous sense our ancestors. He would undoubtedly think in terms of some kind of a god. And his god, I felt sure, was the Spirit of the Rocks.*

Today, we no longer believe in the Spirit of the Rocks. Or if we do, we put the idea rather differently. But we all, willy-nilly and in spite of our conscious selves, have to believe in something. And as the time drew near when I would have to leave the cliff dwelling, it occurred to me that I had been reaching out toward an extension of some such belief when, almost two weeks earlier, I had decided to spend the rest of my time in the Canyon trying to find out what its museum had to say about the species *Homo sapiens*.

But when I tried to assess the results I had to admit that I did not seem to have found what I was looking for, or had imagined I was looking for. I had found the exhibits, all right, clearly labeled. And in the cliff dwelling I had moved back at last inside the museum. But I did not really seem to have discovered a gallery marked "Man." Not, at least, the echoing and fruitful kind of gallery I had found on Beaver Sand Bar. I had failed, in other words, to discover my own Spirit of the Rocks.

But by now I could begin to see that there had never really been much hope of success in this delicate task. For one thing I had been trying to force my journey into the shape I imagined it "ought" to have: I had been thinking instead of letting myself drift. I had also, I saw now, been looking too closely, much as certain creeds and philosophies seem to miss the broader truth by looking too closely at man and ig-

---

*While I lived in his cliff I was quite sure of it. Anthropologists wisely steer clear of this kind of speculation, but one of them remarked to me that as such people tend to have naturalistic religions, my assumption is in a broad sense quite reasonable.

noring his context. There was another reason too for my apparent failure. It had been there for some time now, staring me in the face. All that remained was for my mind to stand back and let certain obvious and quite insistent facts fall into place. But another twenty-four hours would have to pass before I became aware that this was so.

Yet in spite of all these errors and impediments I did not really seem to have missed my longer-term target.*

A year before, when I sat on the lip of the Rim beneath the juniper tree and looked deep into the space and the silence, I had understood, dimly, that one of my reasons for wanting to go down into the Canyon was the hope that by immersing myself in its vastness I might find a way to reconcile the apparent insignificance of man with our own individual and undeniable convictions of vitality—a reconciliation that each of us has at some time to make for himself, alone and anew.

Now, no matter how often we tell ourselves that there is no intellectually discernible purpose in life I think we most of us tend, at some deep level, to keep on attempting our reconciliation—our search for meaning—in terms very close to "purpose." But now I had bypassed this windmill. I accepted that we men, the first product of evolution to become moderately conscious of itself, could hardly expect to understand, yet, the driving force behind the whole immense and unimaginable process. More than likely, anyway,

---

*In trying to write down my thoughts during these final days inside the Canyon it may well be necessary to cheat a little, for I am no longer certain just how much I understood then and how much I came to understand later. You always need time, I suppose, to sort out the meanings of a major experience. But the meanings were already there, I am sure, deep down. It is just that it probably took time for all the verbalized, relatively coherent thoughts to well up onto the surface of my mind.

"purpose" was a mere human concept, inapplicable to the comprehended reality.

But now I had accepted the terrible sweep of geologic time and I had felt, superimposed on the deliberate rhythm of the rocks, the pulse of life and the throb of man. I had glimpsed the way these different arcs of time fitted together, one with the other, interlocking. Above all, I had overcome the fear that lurks somewhere deep in most of us, the fear that comes when somebody first says: "Man is a newcomer on earth," the fear that threatens to overwhelm us when we first look back and down into the huge and horrifying vaults of time that ticked away before man existed. And by overcoming this fear I had freed myself, much as I had freed myself when I swam across the sullen back eddy at the mouth of Havasu Creek.

I had freed myself from our dogmas. Only in my faintest moments could I revert to the vision of man as a being whose valid aim in life is to snuffle around fretting over the future of his individual soul or some similar artifact. Instead, I would see him—and not just intellectually any longer—as a natural and still-moving-forward outgrowth of everything that preceded him, as another quantum in the continuing trajectory of life. I would see each individual man as an organism beginning to emerge from the cushioned realm of instinct into the uncharted and frightful arena of intellect. As an animal still a long way from being rational, but one at last tinged with rationality. As the first animal privileged and condemned to self-awareness. As a creature, therefore, of tears and laughter. As a creature, above all, that was moving forward in the inescapable grip of time—moving forward from the hand-to-mouth existence of simple stone houses and cliff dwellings into richer though more dangerous realms of potential. So for me, now, it would always be "man, the exciting animal." A phenomenon that sometimes, overreaching, scattered metal and corpses, horribly, across silent rock. But a phenomenon that sometimes, reaching out as it must, would fly two shining metal monsters fifty feet apart at almost the speed of sound through a narrow chasm a mile down in the face of the earth, quite needlessly and quite magnificently.

It was moments like this, I saw—glorious mishmash blends of careful intellect and crazy courage—that had put us on top of the heap. That had given us dominion. That had made us, for the time being, the spearhead of life. The spearhead, that was the key. Man turned out to be not so much a newcomer on earth as a new spearhead.

The steady knowledge that you are part of a spearhead is an exhilarating thing; and now the thrust and the excitement and the danger and the potential seemed to me to be more important and more satisfying and certainly more practical than a problematical "purpose." The eons before man emerged were not a terrible void, were not something my mind had to shun. They had become the essence. Without them man was meaningless. Unless he accepted them, a man could not be truly man. Now I accepted them. And the grain of the acceptance was the thing. For mine was not a reluctant acceptance, not a grudging acknowledgment of something I could no longer deny. I accepted gladly. To understand man's significance, I saw, you must first accept his insignificance. Only then could you focus him into importance against his stupendous, unshruggable background. And now, accepting this vision utterly, accepting it without fear and with joy, I had, for the time being at least, found all I needed.

Naturally, it would not always be enough. But the

direction you are moving in is what matters, not the place you happen to be. And for the time being it all looked quite limpidly simple. I was an organism that fitted into the pattern of the man-world and the man-world fitted into the life-world and the life-world fitted into the rock-world and the rock-world fitted into broader domains. That was all. I fitted in. We all fitted in. My journey had left me with this sure grid of meaning to build on, and for the present at least I needed no myths, no symbols.

At noon on the second day I came down from the cliff dwelling and after a while turned westward, away from the river at last, up Nankoweap Creek.

As I walked, the surface of my mind was busy with thoughts of my own immediate future: with routes and water problems and even, vaguely, with coming problems of the outside world. But I must also have been thinking, deeper down, of a wider future. For before long a curious thought crept slyly to the surface.

I was thinking, I imagine, of the rich potential of man. Thinking hopefully of a time that might quite soon come when he learns not merely new knowledge but new humility, and so new wisdom. A time when his know-how will run less rampant and he will learn the value of "feel-how": to balance, to curb, and to inspire. A time when treason will have become a meaningless word and patriotism is judged a crime. A time when he lives in harmony not only with the rest of the animal world but with the rock and rolling hills, with the forests and rivers, with the desert and the oceans and the uncorrupted air—not for any imagined altruistic reason but because he understands that it is the only way he can survive.

It is painfully obvious that this happy condition may abort. For we face a palisade of problems.

Every age no doubt sees itself as pivotal in the history of man. But there seems fairly solid ground for asserting that we live today in a period of profound and critical ferment—of tensions that we can harness or can crumble under. For the human bubble is expanding so fast in size and in complexity and in the new threats it poses to its own existence that many people have come to believe that "something has got to happen soon."

This phrase was apparently what generated the curious thought that crept slyly to the surface of my mind soon after I came down from my cliff dwelling, because I halted for a moment and jotted down in my notebook: "For years now I have felt that there is something wrong with our present concepts of time. A new concept of it could be one of the things that 'is going to happen soon.' "

And then I put my notebook away and walked on westward again beside the clear, down-rushing waters of Nankoweap Creek.*

*In the days since I came up out of the Canyon I have returned quite often to my insubstantial hint about a reordering of the way we think about time. Frankly, I have not been able to do very much with it. But then, as I am sure this book shows, I am ill-equipped for the task. I have very confused ideas of what I mean by "time." Fundamentally, I think I visualize it as some kind of absolute entity that moves inexorably past us; but on a newer and less secure level I am sure that it is more like a pattern through which everything we know about must move.

Not long ago I was cheered to read that a mathematics professor, apparently an expert in the field, had complained in print of "the difficulty of talking sense about time."

I was also heartened to learn that "Pythagoras, when he was asked what time was, answered that it was the soul of this world."

Finally, I stumbled on what I chose to regard as a glimmer of support in the closing chapter of a beautiful and widely read book: "And the angel which I saw stand upon the sea and upon the earth lifted up his hand to heaven, and sware by him that liveth for ever and ever, who created heaven, and the things that therein are, and the earth, and the things that therein are, and the sea, and the things which are therein, that *there should be time no longer:* but in the days of the voice of the seventh angel, when he shall begin to sound, the mystery of God should be finished, as he hath declared to his servants the prophets." (Italics mine, not the angel's.)

EXIT

―――

I WAS washing in Nankoweap Creek when, quite unexpectedly, the world caught up with me.

Ever since Beaver Sand Bar I had been aware in
one sense that it had been moving in on me, this almost forgotten world that presumably still existed out
beyond the Rim. First had come Doug with his news
of outside happenings. Then the crashed airliners and
the helicopter. Then the jets. But none of these disturbances had been quite insistent enough to force me
into a full belief that the other world really existed.
Then I came down from my cliff dwelling.

On the soft surface of a Colorado sand bar, just
below the mouth of Nankoweap Creek, I found two
thin, straight, parallel impressions, about ten feet long
and the same distance apart. And all at once the helicopter was even more real and intrusive than when
I had seen and heard it, back near the crashed airliners. Two sets of footprints, originating at the pontoon
marks, corrupted the smooth sand. Twenty yards
away, a half-eaten orange rocked gently and disgustingly at the water's edge.

A few minutes later I climbed a talus spur that ran

down toward the river. As I reached its crest I heard, unbelieving, the sound of a small motor. It was faint and far off, but undeniable. At first I could see nothing. Then I made out, less than a mile upriver and just beyond the point at which my map showed that the Park boundary crossed the Colorado, a dark speck. It stood out in the river, near the far bank, infinitesimal in that huge world of cliff and space. I lifted my binoculars. The speck jumped into focus as some kind of engineering rig. An A-frame perhaps, or a small derrick. It had the unlikely air of a dredging operation, but in the end I gave up trying to guess its purpose. (It was as well for my peace of mind, I decided later, that I failed to guess.) I just tried to push away the noise and the knowledge of the ugly machine. But even as I did so I knew that they had broken more than the silence.

The third intrusion was in every way a pleasant event. And yet, because its echoes came from my own personal outside world, it was in a way the most insistent. Near the tip of that talus spur that ran down to the Colorado stood a small stone cairn. Inside the cairn I found a rusty can, and inside the can some sheets of paper. They were headed: "DAILY BULLETIN, MONDAY, JULY 4, 1947—NORMAN NEVILL'S COLORADO RIVER EXPEDITION." At its foot the bulletin listed the party's ten members. I read the names with astonishment.

Three of the party were people that I might, I suppose, reasonably have been expected to know. Randall Henderson, compiler of the bulletin, had once been editor of *Desert* magazine, and when I was preparing for my summer's walk up California I had corresponded with him about the lower Colorado. Otis Marston had run the Canyon many times by boat, lived three blocks from my Berkeley apartment, and had supplied information that helped convert my

Canyon dream into reality. Margaret Marston was his wife. But the names that caught my eye were Al and Elma Milotte. The Milottes are a famous husband-and-wife Walt Disney nature photography team. One day in 1951, when I was living on a hill that overlooked Lake Nakuru in Kenya, their gray four-wheel-drive Dodge camper pulled up, unannounced, outside the house. I was alone at the time. The Milottes, after asking permission, slapped up a tripod and photographed the vast flocks of flamingoes that turned the shores of the lake, mile after mile, into a three-hundred-foot strip of delicate and breathtaking pink. Afterward I offered "British coffee, if you can face it," and the Milottes laughed and said eagerly that if I could provide hot water they would, if I really didn't mind, make their own Nescafé. So we sat and talked, looking out over the pink-fringed lake. Before they left, the Milottes said that if I ever went to America I must be sure to look them up in Hollywood. I left Africa for good soon afterward, and for seven years now I had lived less than half the length of California away from Hollywood; but somehow I had never done anything about the Milottes' invitation. And now, here we were, meeting at the mouth of Nankoweap Creek. It was a surprisingly real meeting. Quite a jolt, in its way. The associations were entirely pleasant; but as I read the folded and faded bulletin I found that the outside world—my own personal outside world—had suddenly become more real than it had been at any moment since the day I climbed up out of Supai.

I am a slow understander. There is often an appreciable time lag before quite obvious facts get through to me. And it was not until late that evening, as I stood washing myself comprehensively in Nankoweap Creek and at the same time worrying away at the details of how much food and water I ought to carry up Nankoweap Trail, that the cumulative weight of the intrusions took effect.

It was only then, with the clear, cool water swirling around my ankles, that I understood at last that the intrusions were what had finally wrecked my already too-conscious attempt to find a gallery marked "Man." Ever since Beaver Sand Bar the outside world had been pressing in—the presumably real other world beyond the Rim. And that kind of world could not exist alongside my kind of museum.

Once I understood what had happened, I knew what was going to happen. Back on Beaver Sand Bar I had decided, a shade self-consciously, that when I reached the North Rim I would, before rejoining civilization, hole up for two or three days in some quiet and commanding eyrie. I would do nothing but contemplate the Canyon and meditate. And I would attain, I felt sure, a pyramid of perception. But now, washing in Nankoweap Creek, I saw quite unexpectedly that it was not going to work out that way. To my surprise, I no longer wanted to resist the world.

I sat down beside the creek and wrote one of the rare passages in my notebook that makes some kind of sense in the original form:

Yes, get out is the thing—It has been a wonderful life—effort, then perception—peace and insight—deer mice and beavers; sunshine and river. But now, washing my head in Nankoweap Creek, I know it is over. I have overstayed my welcome in the museum. The things I wanted to do are done. The time has passed for contemplation. I must get out and do. For doing is what counts. The contemplation is only for that.

And all at once I realized with a jolt, in a new and hard and certain way, that my journey was almost over.

For a long time I stayed sitting there beside the creek, letting the sun dry me off (it was over 100 degrees now, even in the shade), and I found myself beginning to list—haphazardly and not at first very seriously—the things I had gained from the journey. I had won a nickel from Harvey Butchart. I had shed twenty surplus pounds and had refined my body to such a peak of fitness that when I went to bed the smoothness of my skin sometimes gave me a woman-thrill. I had gained a sense of old fears overcome. I had learned that life begins at forty-one: after four sad years in which everything around me had been flat and gray, the world was once again round and shining—rounder and more splendid than it had ever been. And I was beginning to understand too that the journey had conferred on me a rare but simple gift: an almost perfect confluence of what I thought and what I felt. Had offered me, that is, the key to contentment.

And almost all the early promises had been fulfilled. For example, when I looked up now at the huge expanse of cracked and weathered rock above Nankoweap Creek, all looking as if it would come crashing down at any minute, it occurred to me that in two months I had heard the sounds of only three small rock fragments. And I felt no surprise. The rhythm of the rocks had long ago become a sure component of my understanding.

Naturally, not everything had turned out the way I had expected. On that first calm evening of the journey, when I camped on the floor of Hualpai Canyon, I had looked up at the silhouetted canyon walls and had pictured the layer on layer of wind-blown sand that had created the sandstone more than 200 million years before and had wondered how soon I would understand the full meaning of "200 million years." Ever since the day I walked down Bass Trail I had accepted, quite naturally and without effort, that the sand had drifted into place, grain by windblown grain, more than 200 million years ago. Yet when I put the original question to myself I had to admit that I still did not really grasp the huge, intrinsic meaning of "200 million years." But now, I found, it did not matter. I knew, accurately and without surprise, how this huge span of time fitted into the earth's history. And that, it had turned out, was all that really mattered.

I saw now that many other things about the journey had not turned out quite as I had expected. The idea of inviting Doug along for the finale to help me reconcile fact and feeling had failed quite dismally. And I had learned almost nothing from the fossils— those ancient messages from which we later forms of life are now deciphering, piece by piece, the story of life's progress down the ages. Nor had I really learned anything from the simpler forms of life, from the algae and the lichens. Intellectually, of course, I had not learned very much at all. I had learned, I mean, precious few hard, objective facts.

But I knew quite certainly, without yet grasping the details, that I had found almost everything I had hoped to find. For a while the rolling cadences of geologic time had been as real to me as our frantic human stutterings. Perhaps even more real. Already that awareness had lost its edge. But it would never quite fade away. When I needed the guidelines they would always be there, a part of my background of understanding. For I had learned, deep down and surely, what I had before understood only intellectually and dimly: that everything we know about is dancing, at its own tempo, to the same overriding rhythm. Mysteries remained, half seen, quarter understood. But they were necessary mysteries. There are rhythms of existence we cannot yet hope to hear.

And all at once I remembered an insight of Emerson's that I had read just before I began my journey: *There is a relation between the hours of our life and the centuries of time.... The hours should be instructed by the ages, and the ages explained by the hours.* Not once in all my weeks in the Canyon had I recalled these words. But now they sounded immeasurably truer. For I had moved around on my own to Emerson's conclusion. And now I knew what to do about it. You cannot escape the age you live in: you are a product of it. You have to stand back from time to time and get your perspectives right. But then you have to come back and resume the task of contributing in your own way to your own age. And this was why the world had suddenly caught up with me. I had seen the ages; now it was time to come back to the hours. It was time to use what I had seen. Time to apply the ages to the frail, overwhelmingly important little time span that was my life, that is all our individual lives. It was time to be out and doing. Out and contributing. For me, that meant out and sharing: out and grappling with the huge task of trying to write down something of what I had found.

I felt sure now that my new understandings had made me fitter for the outside world. Had made me a fitter contributor. For from now on I would understand, almost always, that the "here and now" is only a flickering heartbeat in many long, slow pulsations. No single thing I saw ought to look totally unimportant. Given time for reflection and the suppression of

prejudice, I would at least have a try at fitting everything into the web of meaning.*

At this point my mind came back to the present—
came back with an awareness of finality to my naked
and now thoroughly dry body sitting beside Nankoweap Creek. At first I felt dissatisfied. It seemed untidy and even invalid to draw the curtains over my
journey on such a small and intensely personal note.
Then I found I was not really unhappy that it should
have turned out that way. There is a powerful human
compulsion to leave things tied up in neat little bundles. But every journey except your last has an open
end. And any journey of value is above all a chapter
in a personal odyssey. Its end is not so much a goal
attained as another point in a continuing process. And
the important thing at the end of a journey—or of a
book—is to keep moving forward, refreshed, with as
little pause as possible.

The Nankoweap Basin is as magnificent in its way
as anything in the Canyon. But when I left the creek
next evening and began the long, waterless, mile-high
climb toward the North Rim I was desperately impa-
tient to be out and doing; and most of the moments I
remember from the final two days of my journey did
not really come from the Canyon.

It was midmorning. Already I had climbed three
thousand feet above Nankoweap Creek. At one of my

*Soon after I left the Canyon I read, in an otherwise unsuccinct paper
on ecology: "Organisms themselves are relatively transient entities through
which materials and energy flow and eventually return to the environment."

In my more skittish moments I am currently inclined to think that I
would rather like this sentence as my epitaph.

regular hourly rests I leaned contentedly against my pack and looked back over Nankoweap Canyon, across the Gorge of the Colorado, toward the South Rim. And all at once I found that I could look out over the Rim. It was the first time in two months that I had seen anything outside the Canyon—the first time I had known in a direct sense that anything else existed. All I could see was an immense plain. It stretched away to the horizon, flat and gray and endless. Just for a moment, the sight unnerved me.

I climbed on. Once, in midafternoon, a sad thought came. In my notebook I scribbled: "Oh dear, for a while now any other countryside is going to look dull."

In late afternoon I passed a Park boundary sign, and a little later it occurred to me quite casually that I had just accomplished what I set out to do: I had traveled on foot from one end of Grand Canyon National Park to the other. It did not seem to mean very much. The journey had succeeded for quite different reasons.

I made my last camp at sunset on the lip of a broad plateau, a thousand feet short of the North Rim. As I sat eating dinner I watched the Canyon's shapes sink down and away into the solid black velvet that I remembered from back along the Esplanade. But now, far out beyond the South Rim, the pulsating lights of a small town interrupted the night. I looked at them with mild surprise. In two months I had forgotten lights.

When I woke next morning a broad red band lay heavy along the eastern horizon. Already the black velvet had moved over into blue. Soon the shapes began. The red band diminished. The sun rose and broadcast thin, tentative beams. Two ravens planed past, craaaking; a woodpecker embarked on its day's bayoneting. The blue velvet eased over into gray. The shapes hardened into buttes and ridges. At last, almost imperceptibly, the gray velvet had become the Canyon.

It was very beautiful. Yet I found, a little sadly, that the birth of this final day had not really inspired me as it should have done, and it occurred to me that perhaps I was sated with beauty and grandeur. The world is not, unfortunately, all beauty or all grandeur. And what I needed now, as a corrective, was some ugliness and some pettiness. I would drive home, I decided, through Las Vegas.

After breakfast I climbed on toward the Rim. Almost at once I moved in among green trees. But soon the trees and the cool shade ended and I was walking among stark, black skeletons. After the first ugly shock I felt less anger than I usually do at a recent burn. Already grass and aspens had sprung up. There were flowers too, blue and scarlet and exquisite. A few more years and this would be a beautiful place. I happened to know that the burn had been caused by a lightning strike, three years before; and now, as I walked, I saw and understood that this forest had over the centuries grown to the stage at which a natural force like lightning could destroy it; and it had been destroyed. The burn was part of a rotation, a cycle, a natural process. It was the first time I had looked at a burn this way. And suddenly I knew that I would see even Las Vegas as part of a process.

The devastation ended. I moved back into green forest. It was a higher forest now, and rich. I trod on a soft carpet of needles, breathed pine-scented air.

Two hours later, still in thick, cool forest, I climbed up onto the North Rim. It should have been the end, but it was not. Soon I came to a fire road. There were tracks in its dust, my first car tracks since I walked down and away from Hualpai Hilltop. Another hour, and I could see a paved road ahead. Sunlight flashed on a row of automobiles. Reluctant now, but still eager, I walked toward them. They were modern automobiles, streamlined by time and the erosion of man's ingenuity into low, sleek creatures that reflected their relationship to the Model T as little, and as much, as we modern men reflect our relationship to the ape.

I stepped out of the trees onto pavement and walked toward the cars. People were moving among them. Ordinary, everyday people.

A man ran his eye over my battered pack and smiled and said: "Having yourself a good time?"

"Yes, thanks," I said, and smiled back.

My journey was over. I had rejoined the present.

EPILOGUE

A carelessness of life and beauty marks
the glutton, the idler and the fool in
their deadly path across history.
—JOHN MASEFIELD

UNLESS WE do something about it, you and I, we may soon find that this book has become a requiem for Grand Canyon.

A few weeks after I came up out of the Canyon I went—acting on a tip from Doug Powell—to a conference on the Pacific Southwest Water Plan. I was horrified at what I heard. I heard a hundred or so engineers—understandably fascinated by a titanic professional challenge, and just as understandably eager to safeguard their jobs for many years to come—debating precise details of how to tear out the guts of the Canyon I had known. Long before the end of the meeting I realized that these competent little men had no grasp at all of what they were proposing to do to the earth.

The Pacific Southwest Water Plan proposes, as a small segment of its whole, three major projects in Grand Canyon; two dams and a tunnel. The United States Bureau of Reclamation consistently soft-pedals the tunnel project, but it is one of the safest political bets of all time that if we allow Congress to sanction the dams, then the tunnel project will within a very few years rerear its ugly head.

It is important to understand the limits of the present proposals. None of the actual structures would lie inside the National Park. Not quite. And the dams would not, as some overeager objectors seem to have suggested, "flood out" Grand Canyon. (Unfortunately, the cult of conservation can blind a man almost as effectively as can the cult of engineering.) If the dams and the tunnel were built, in fact, the Canyon would not, from the Rim, *look* so very different. But the heart of the place would be gone.*

The living river—the superb mechanism that has created the Canyon—would vanish. At best it would become a loosely connected chain of dead lakes; at worst, a dried-out channel. For the forty-five-mile-long tunnel would divert all—or all but a trickle—of the Colorado for most of its length through the Park. The beaver would die. So would most of the bronze, pink-finned carp. And the whole delicate, interlocking web of life that draws its sap from the river would be ripped apart. Further downstream, a ninety-three-mile-long reservoir backing up behind a dam at Bridge Canyon (which would be the tallest dam in the Western Hemisphere) would drown the entire river channel of Grand Canyon National Monument and would penetrate thirteen miles into the Park. At the mouth of Havasu Creek, the black, mussel-mosaic ledge along which I had made my reconnaissance would lie buried under eighty-five feet of slack and lifeless water.

*We are inclined to forget that sight is in some ways the most superficial of our senses. Immediately after I came out of the Canyon I flew low over the whole of my route. It was an interesting experience. But that was all. Sight was the only sense I could use. And the difference between flying over Grand Canyon and living in it is like the difference between, on the one hand, seeing a beautiful woman in a bikini and, on the other, making deeply satisfying love to her, with all her warmth and smoothness and fragrance and murmurings and movement.

From time to time the reservoir would recede and leave a hideous band of silt and scum along the ruined rockwalls.

But these are examples of only the obvious, measurable havoc. The plan would breed even greater tragedies: the annulment of untrammeled space; the casual cancellation of solitude and silence; the rape, that is, of the museum.

On a microcosmic scale, the invasion has already begun. The A-frame or derrick that I saw near the cliff dwellings, a few meticulous yards outside the boundary of the National Park, was engaged in exploration work for a small surge-dam, about fifty feet high, that would be a water-level-controlling accessory to one of the main dams, twelve miles upriver in Marble Canyon. Once construction began at the surge-dam site there would be more than a single helicopter servicing it (as was the one I saw) and making ghoulish forays down to the crashed airliners and corrupting smooth sand bars with pontoon marks and leaving half-eaten oranges to rock gently and disgustingly at the water's edge.

But such intrusions would be insignificant compared with what was to come. There would be an access road, for one thing, and probably a huge heap of rubble from a tunnel for the road. All around the dam site, bulldozers and dynamite would rip and tear at rock and bush and sand bar. And the scars would remain. For the desert, unlike most kinds of country, takes centuries rather than decades to veil the inhumanities of man.

From this small dam site (and from all the major and subsidiary sites of the plan) there would pour into the emasculated river—to lodge and drift and lodge again—all the inevitable filth and feces of construction: diesel fuel, discarded oil filters, rags, paper, beer cans. Even when the construction of the surge-dam was over, that place would never again be the same. The cliff dwellings—though open now to the atrocities of feeble-minded, scribbling Kilroys—would still be there, three quarters of a mile downriver. But only as curiosities. They would no longer exist in a world that space and silence and solitude had set richly apart from the present.

It would be the same elsewhere in the Canyon. According to present plans, spoil from the tunnel would be excreted from side shafts. At least one of these shafts would vent inside the Park, and it is all too easy to imagine the bedlam let loose as a cavalcade of trucks dumped a gigantic mound of dust and rubble in some remote sanctuary like Kwagunt Basin. The power plant at the tunnel's exit (not to mention a 470-foot dam across a sidecanyon) is presently programmed for the Inner Gorge just below the three superbly savage and silent amphitheaters that Harvey Butchart had probably been the first man to cross; just below the place at which I had seen through swirling cloud my first green and dignified bighorn sheep—members of a species so devoted to solitude that it will not even tolerate the presence of a few wild horses within its broad territory. Below this place would come first the din and destruction and irremediable scarring of construction work, then humming turbines and a permanent access road (through some sleight of past political hand, the north side of the river at this point lies outside the Park). If the power plant is built, helicopters will assuredly service it. Will service it copiously. And because man is, thank God, an inquisitive animal, the pilots will make forbidden and therefore doubly challenging landings out on the Esplanade and along the now silent terrace that swings around to Fossil Bay. Meanwhile, down at the other end of the Esplanade, raucous powerboats will be trailing water skiers eighty-five feet above the grave of Havasu Creek.

Now, please do not misunderstand me. I find water skiing an exhilarating sport. But Grand Canyon is no more the place for it than is the Louvre for roller skating. Few people would condone a roller derby in that man-made museum; but as Joseph Wood Krutch has pointed out: "When a man despoils a work of art we call him a vandal, when he despoils a work of nature we call him a developer."

If the engineers are unleashed to do their "developing,"* the Canyon will still, as I say, look very much

---

*As this book goes to press (summer, 1967), we are being told that Grand Canyon has been "saved." This is simply not the case. Not yet.

Thanks to a huge public outcry, the tunnel project has now been stuffed deep underground; and the federal administration has recently withdrawn its plans for the upper dam, in Marble Canyon. But Arizona and other concerned states remain free to reintroduce this project in Congress. In fact, one such bill has already been introduced.

The question of the lower dam has been turned over to the judgment of Congress. And already talk is buzzing around House and Senate of a new bill to authorize the renamed Hualpai Dam in Bridge Canyon. This is the dam that would back up a ninety-three-mile reservoir and drown the entire river channel within Grand Canyon National Monument. (This magnificent and presently untouched gorge is often run by boat parties. Last spring I managed to find a way through on foot, with some river-assists from my air mattress; and I can assure you that it is an awe-inspiring place.) The reservoir, as I have said, would penetrate thirteen miles into the National Park. According to present unofficial plans, Congress would attempt to excise these thirteen miles from the Park. In exchange for this loss and for the inundation in the National Monument, the bill would add to the Park the upper part of the Canyon that would have included Marble Dam.

Now such a plan makes good sense to a politician. He calls it "reasonable compromise"—and believes what he says.

But people determined to conserve the beauties and harmonies of the earth will reject any such suggestion. In fact, they are now campaigning to include within an enlarged National Park the whole three hundred river-miles of Grand Canyon, from Lee's Ferry to Lake Mead. And the opposing politicians are already accusing them of "being unwilling to accept a reasonable compromise."

Now, compromise is, very properly, the essence of a politician's life. But when he asks a conservationist to accept only one dam in Grand Canyon instead of two, he is in no sense proposing a compromise. He is acting like a man out in wild country who feels the first pangs of hunger and who, ignoring rich sources of food around him, proposes a plan to his sole human companion; and who, when the companion objects, says: "All right, then. I won't cut off both your legs. I'll only cut off one. That should satisfy me for a while." (For Update on all this, see page 240.)

the same from the Rim. But its magic will have gone. The story of the earth will still be there, written in the rocks; but the Canyon will no longer be a huge, uninterrupted, enveloping world of space and solitude and silence.

The silence will be the most certain and the most tragic loss: the silence that I met face to face, like something solid, in the first moment I stood on the Rim; the silence that encompassed me and caressed and soothed my mind and carried me out beyond my own time to a new sense of inclusion with rock and beaver and rattlesnake and sandfly until in the end I became, quite naturally, a part of the terrestrial plot. And without this envelope of silence the Grand Canyon of the Colorado will no longer be a vast natural museum of the earth's history. It will no longer be a museum at all.

I suggest that we little men have no damned right even to consider such vandalism—for any reason at all.

And the reason the engineers give for what they want to do to the Canyon is illuminating.

They do not pretend that their dams would conserve water. In fact, increased evaporation from the reservoirs would waste enough water to supply a city bigger than Boston.

And the dams and tunnel are not designed to produce necessary power. Some play has been made with the notion that their power will soon be needed for the growing population of the Southwest. But this seems a specious argument for men fully aware that cheaper power will almost certainly become available within a very few years. It is an even more curious argument for men who must surely know not only that "planning for growth is a cause of growth" but also that one of man's most imperative tasks right now is to smother his population explosion.

The prime and brazen reason for building the dams and the tunnel is, as I say, illuminating: the task of these structures is to produce power that will raise enough money to make other sectors of the Pacific Southwest Water Plan more economically acceptable. (In fact, it might be more accurate to say: "The dams are being proposed merely to make the plan politically palatable in terms of the budget systems traditionally employed by state and federal governments.") Strip away the fancy talk, in other words, and you find that Grand Canyon museum is to be sacrificed so that we can have cheaper bath water. Or perhaps—because much of the water is used for agriculture—it might be better to say: "so that we can have cheaper broccoli."

Naturally, it is not much use trying to dissuade the engineers by talking about such intangibles as a museum of the kind I mean. In order to function, engineers must be able to measure their materials; and you can't assign a dollars-per-capita value to space or to solitude. Neither can you measure silence on a slide rule—except as zero decibels, and that misses the point with a quite consummate engineering skill. So the task of saving Grand Canyon—and the principle of inviolate National Parks—is up to those who can think in different terms. After all, we do not judge the glory that was Greece in terms of Gross National Product. And I doubt if America will be judged by the price of its bath water—or its broccoli.

I was able to make my journey through Grand Canyon only because of people who thought in terms different from these. People like President Teddy Roosevelt. Roosevelt stood on the Rim and looked and said: "Leave it as it is. You cannot improve on it. The ages have been at work on it, and man can only mar it." Soon afterward he established by proclamation Grand Canyon National Monument.

Whether our sons and daughters and their sons and daughters will be able to make the kind of journey I was able to make—or, almost as important, whether they will have, always, the rich possibility of making such a journey—depends on us. We do not have to build a Parthenon. Nor to create any work of art. We face a greater and perhaps almost as difficult task: to shield from the blind fury of material "progress" a work of time that is unique on the surface of our earth. And we shall be judged, you and I, by what we did or failed to do.

UPDATE: 1989

THE PLACE

The simple geologic scenario outlined on page 3 is no longer the current scientific "truth." Most geologists now believe that more complicated events occurred. For our purposes, though, this evolution of belief alters nothing.

EPILOGUE

After due thought, I am letting the original Epilogue stand. True, the old engineering threats to Grand Canyon have receded: the National Park has been extended to include the whole river from Lee's Ferry to Lake Mead—and although some Arizona politicians refuse to give up, national parks seem for the moment to be unassailable. But a threat unforeseen twenty years ago has emerged. The downstream effects of Glen Canyon Dam appear to be dislocating riverside life within the Canyon, and a political war is now raging over the rhythms of water release from the dam. In other words, the battleground has shifted but the war goes on.

So not too much has really changed. Almost every day new plans surface for a dam or other massive engineering project in some unspoiled place. My warning at the end of the footnote on page 237, about the nature of political "compromise," stands rocklike. The price of wilderness still includes eternal vigilance.

C.F., *March 1989*

APPENDIX

———

*Indicates items replaced at each cache and airdrop.
†Indicates items replaced at certain caches and/or airdrops.

EQUIPMENT LIST:

	Pounds	Ounces
Pack, complete (frame, bag, harness, waist belt)	4	13
Walking staff (bamboo)		14

CLOTHING

	Pounds	Ounces
Boots (Italian)	5	12
†3 pairs socks (wool, nylon-reinforced)		15
Moccasins—for wear around camp		9
Shorts (corduroy)	1	9
Long pants (whipcord; not carried second half of journey)	1	10
Belt (leather)		4
†1 pair undershorts		2
Shirt		12
Hat		4
Scarf		1
Poncho/groundsheet/sun awning		14

	Pounds	Ounces
Down-filled jacket	1	1
†1 bandana		1

SLEEPING GEAR

	Pounds	Ounces
Sleeping bag (mummy-type; down-filled; nylon shell)	2	11
Air mattress (hip-length rubber-coated canvas)	1	14
Air-mattress patch kit		2

KITCHEN UTENSILS

	Pounds	Ounces
2 nesting cooking pots (aluminum; 2½, 3½ pints)	1	4
Stove (Svea 123, gasoline-burning), with ⅓ pint gas	1	7
*White gas container (aluminum; 1⅛ pint capacity)	1	3
Funnel for white gas		⅛
Stainless-steel Sierra Club cup		3
Spoon		2
Sheath knife		6
Carborundum stone		1
Salt-and-pepper container		2
Sugar container (polyethylene)		2
Powdered milk container (squeezer, nozzle-tipped)		1
*Powdered detergent container (polyethylene)		
empty		1
full		5
Miniature can opener (Army-type)		⅛
*7 bookmatches		1
Waterproof matchsafe (wooden matches; needle and thread)		1

	Pounds	*Ounces*
2 aluminum canteens (½ gallon; screw tops, felt-covered)		
empty	1	10
full	10	2
2 plastic canteens (just under ½ gallon; polyethylene)		
empty		14
full	8	8
Auxiliary canteen—for drawing water from shallow rainpockets (baby bottle, 250 cc.)		
empty		1
full	1	2

FOOD (ONE WEEK'S RATIONS; ALL WEIGHTS ARE GROSS)

	Pounds	*Ounces*
*Mixed dry cereal	1	0
*7 packages vacuum-dried fruit (4 ounces each)	1	13
*8 packages dried soup (Maggi)	1	7
*5 bars Wilson's Meat Food Product (pemmican)	1	0
*2 bars Wilson's Bacon		7
*Dehydrated potatoes	1	9
*Dehydrated beans		8
*Dehydrated mixed vegetables		4
*Granulated sugar	1	8
*Powdered non-fat milk	1	0
*30 tea bags		3
*Dry raisins	1	0
*Semi-sweet chocolate		9
*3½ bars mintcake candy	1	6
†2 packages fruit drink mix		4
*Salt		3
†Salt tablets (in 35-mm. film can)		2
*Rum fudge bar (Horlicks; emergency ration)		8
*1 can menu-varying goodies (oysters, frogs' legs, cocktail meatballs, mixed appetizers; not carried)		
*1 small bottle claret (not carried)		

PHOTOGRAPHIC EQUIPMENT, ETC.

	Pounds	*Ounces*
Binoculars		14
35-mm. camera (first half of journey; Ansco Super Regent; replaced halfway by Zeiss Contaflex)	2	7
Exposure meter		6
Telescopic tripod		14
Flash bracket—for binocular attachment		3
Lens brush		1
*3 or, sometimes, 4 rolls 35-mm. color film (Kodachrome X)		12
Sunlight filter (both cameras); close-up attachments (for Zeiss camera)		3

SUNDRIES

	Pounds	*Ounces*
White polyethylene sheet, 9 × 5 feet— for waterproofing gear on river crossings, sun awning, and airdrop marker (carried on reconnaissance and second half of journey only)	1	0
"Office"—specially made waterproof-fabric envelope, zippered, holding: †onionskin paper for notes, †1 roll cellotape, †rubber bands, paperback book, †Moleskins for feet, scissors, mirror (for signaling), †spare sunglasses, pens and pencils, pack patching sheet.	1	5
2 copies each of two U.S. Geological Survey maps of Grand Canyon		12
†Notebook		2
Pocket thermometer		1
Toilet articles (facecloth, ½ bar soap, toothbrush, comb, †hand lotion)		6
*1 roll toilet paper		7
*Rubbing alcohol for feet (in plastic bottle)		5
†Foot powder		4

	Pounds	Ounces
Fly dope		1
First-aid kit (roll adhesive tape, roll gauze, Anacin tablets, antibiotic ointment)		5
Knee "Ace" bandages (also used as puttees)		4
Snakebite suction kit (Cutter)		1
†Coconut oil (in 35-mm. film can)		1
†Halazone (water-purifying) tablets		¼
Flashlight, with batteries		7
*Spare long-life batteries		4
Spare pack fittings		2
Prospector's magnifying glass		2
Compass		5
Hanks of braided nylon cord		4
Coil of ¼-inch nylon rope	1	14
Belt clip		1
Fishing tackle (spool of 6-pound nylon, several BB shot, eyed hooks)		½
†Salmon eggs (in 35-mm. film can)		1
*Spare plastic freezer bags (which were used in large quantities for wrapping almost everything)		1
Eyeglasses with case		6
†Sunglasses (for spares, see "Office" item above)		1

Note: No meaningful figure is reached by totaling the individual weights, partly because not all items were carried at once, partly because weights of most items are correct only to nearest ounce. On the only occasion on which the pack was weighed—immediately before departure from Supai, with a full week's food and full 2-gallon load of water—it turned the scale at 66½ pounds.

A NOTE ABOUT THE AUTHOR

Colin Fletcher was born in Wales and educated in England. After six years' World War II service in the Royal Marines, he went to East Africa in 1947, farmed for four years in Kenya and later surveyed and built a road over a virgin mountain in Southern Rhodesia (now Zimbabwe). In the 1950s he crossed the Atlantic and prospected—among other pursuits—in northern and western Canada. In 1956 he moved south to California. Soon afterward he spent a summer walking from Mexico to Oregon across California's deserts and mountains. Later he became the first man known to have walked the length of Grand Canyon National Park within the Canyon's rim. Each of these feats generated a book: *The Thousand-Mile Summer* and *The Man Who Walked Through Time*. Mr. Fletcher continues to walk—and to write books: *The Complete Walker* (revised twice), *The Winds of Mara, The Man from the Cave,* and *The Secret Worlds of Colin Fletcher.*